# THEY'RE JUST NOT INTERESTED

# THEY'RE JUST NOT INTERESTED

# THEY'RE JUST NOT INTERESTED

## REDISCOVERING OUR FAITH AND APPROACHING NONBELIEVERS WITH THE FAITH OF A WRESTLER

BY MICHAEL FESSLER

BANYAN PRESS

THEY'RE JUST NOT
INTERESTED

Banyan Press™

Rosemount, MN

©2016 Michael Fessler. All rights reserved

No part of this book may be reproduced, stored in a retrieval system, or transmitted by any means without the written permission of the author.

Scriptures taken from the Holy Bible, New International Version®, NIV®. Copyright © 1973,1978,1984,2011 by Biblica, Inc.™ Used by permission of Zondervan. All rights reserved worldwide. www.zondervan.com The "NIV" and "New International Version" are trademarks registered in the United States Patent and Trademark Office by Biblica, Inc.™ All rights reserved.

First published by Banyan Press in 2016

ISBN: 978-0-692-76081-9 (sc)

Printed in the United States of America

Cover image by Michael Fessler

Any imagery or design in the interior of this book provided by cliparts.co/page-divider

Because of the dynamic nature of the internet, any web addresses or links contained in this book may have changed since publication and may no longer be valid.

Dedicated to my bride, Kristin

THEY'RE JUST NOT INTERESTED

# CONTENTS

| | |
|---|---|
| **FOREWORD – DAN RUSSELL** | 9 |
| **PREFACE** | 11 |
| INTRODUCTION | 15 |
| CHAPTER 1: STILL DEALING WITH THE ENLIGHTENMENT | 29 |
| CHAPTER 2: THE CROSS IS FOOLISHNESS | 51 |
| CHAPTER 3: THE FAITH OF A WRESTLER | 64 |
| CHAPTER 4: JESUS THE WRESTLER | 81 |
| CHAPTER 5: WRESTLING AND RELATIONSHIP | 92 |
| CHAPTER 6: FAMILY | 106 |
| CHAPTER 7: THIS IS LIFE | 123 |
| CHAPTER 8: THE PASSION OF THE CHRIST | 132 |
| CHAPTER 9: LAMENT | 139 |

CHAPTER 10: THE BEAUTY OF SIMPLICITY   150

CHAPTER 11: THIS LIFE MATTERS   157

CONCLUSION   171

**ABOUT THE AUTHOR**   176

# FOREWORD

I am thankful for Michael Fessler, the wrestler, who dares to struggle with the deeper things in the wrestling match of life. His newest book invites you into the struggle to get to the heart of a life with Jesus. There are powerful personal stories that beautifully portray his wrestling through theology and doctrine to grabbing a hold of faith that matters. Michael Fessler offers transparent insight into his own suffering that has taught him deeper truths into life with God.

This book is an honest conversation into the beauty of the deeper discoveries found in difficulties we face on this side of eternity. He engages the reader to confront religion and re-evaluate the life giving purpose of God's greater engagement. This book helps to refocus, re-engage and renew a life producing faith compelling us to push beyond religion into a restored passionate faith in Jesus.

If you are on this side of eternity, you will be faced with battles. It is in this struggle where suffering intersects with the sacred. This book helps to re-discover the greatness and goodness of God in the wrestling match of life. Life is a wrestling match and everyone wrestles. The reader catches a glimpse of one man's struggle to understand the beauty found in the battle. Michael Fessler has entered the ring and he invites the reader to do the same.

Wrestling for Him,

Dan Russell

*Lead Pastor of Battle Ground Foursquare Church in Battle Ground, Washington.*

*Author of the book "Finish Strong: The Dan Russell Story."*

# PREFACE

Several years ago I set out on a journey that led me to publish my previous book – *Faith and Wrestling: How the Role of a Wrestler Mirrors the Christian Life*. The journey was exciting, for sure! In fact, the success of the book enabled me to establish some great relationships with people from around the country, and to my surprise, around the world. The book was not a 'New York Times Best Seller,' and it didn't garner attention via national news media, either. But with the messages and e-mails I received from readers communicating that the book had impacted their life in a tremendous way, I experienced a great deal of satisfaction as well as affirmation that publishing my work was worthwhile. The book revealed a message I discovered as a former competitor in the sport of wrestling and as a person who has lived the vast majority of his life as a follower of Jesus. Moreover, I was engrossed in the world of theology during my studies at Bethel University, and it was during this time that the premise of the book came to life.

After the book's publication – after more thought and reflection, speaking engagements, and so on – I realized something potentially profound. That is, perhaps the idea of 'faith and wrestling' isn't just a message for those Christians who have experienced life as a wrestling competitor. Maybe wrestling is reflective of the Christian faith as a whole. And if this is true, what would this mean for the church?

As I surveyed the world around me – particularly my own culture here in America – I noticed something rather unfortunate. That is, there appears to be a disconnect between the contemporary, American culture and the established method of the church in promulgating the Christian gospel. In short, it seems we have developed into a community of people obsessed with intellectualism, as if we need to prove to others that we're not ignorant. Or if it's not a conveyed intellectualism, it's an assumed position of suggesting we have an answer to everything. Instead of living as a group of people humbly chasing after God, engaging the spiritually lost with the magnificence of God's gospel, and wrestling with the struggles and difficulties we face as human beings, we seem to be living as those who think we have it all figured out.

As you'll discover throughout the course of this book, and my own personal journey revealed in it, I believe the "faith of a wrestler" to be the most accurate description and approach to the Christian faith. Christians are those who have wrestled with God and what He means, and have put their faith and trust in Him through the person of Jesus Christ.

Of course, proper acknowledgment and gratitude regarding things of this nature must include God first and foremost. It is the heart of God which is the goal of this work, and I sincerely believe that He places these passions and desires within us to know Him more deeply.

I would also like to thank my wife, Kristin. She doesn't typically enjoy practices in theological discourse, but when she engages these discussions her thoughts help me see things a little more clearly and practically. She has played a significant part in helping me identify the beauty and simplicity of God's gospel.

Thank you to Terry Hancock, Freddy Corona, Sally Ness, Molly Grabowski, Dan Vallimont, Jack Spates, Mark Palmer, and all the other readers of the preliminary manuscript who provided relevant feedback which resulted in the finished product of this book.

Thank you to everyone who takes the initiative to read this book and who, upon reading it, finds it valuable enough to share with others. Perhaps you'll discover that the faith of a wrestler accurately reflects your own faith. And if so, maybe sharing this book with others will help them to discover the very same thing.

# THEY'RE JUST NOT INTERESTED

# INTRODUCTION

When I was a young boy, I would to talk to God as if He was standing right next to me. Or if He wasn't standing next to me, I imagined He had no difficulty in hearing me from some location in the sky. For me, God was always personal – not a distant being sitting atop the universe without a care in the world. He was so personal, in fact, that I felt as if He was literally walking through time with me.

    I accepted Jesus into my life (as they say) at the age of six. I still remember walking up to the pastor with my mom after the service and telling him that I wanted to follow Jesus. The strange thing is that, even though I barely understood what I was doing or the decision I was making, my heart seemed to know enough for me. As a six year old, my theology was virtually nonexistent. My mind wasn't even capable of wrapping itself around the theological concepts and doctrines inherent in the faith, nor did I know or care about the debates in theology that have been recurrent in the church. And it's strange, because it's as if it didn't matter in the grand scheme of things. From that moment on, my life belonged to Jesus. My mind had little to do with the decision. I wasn't engaged in a pursuit of deep philosophical thought or on a journey to discover the meaning of life. My response to God's call to follow Him was a mere prompting of the heart. I admit that there was something supernatural about the whole thing. Not only did my heart convince my mind – which didn't need much convincing to begin with – but as I grew older, as I experienced the world and all of its pain alongside its goodness, my mind, though it questioned many things, never questioned the realness of Jesus and the salvation discovered through Him. The truth of it was certain to me.

Conversation with God was a natural part of my everyday life. I suppose an outsider may have thought that I was an early case of schizophrenia – talking to myself so often, even answering questions that I myself posed. But the truth is that, regardless of it being particularly strange or not, I was communicating with God. And it's not that He had an audible voice, providing clear answers to my questions. To be certain, I *do* believe that I heard Him speak to me at times through my heart and conscience. But even when He didn't (which was most of the time) I would talk to Him anyways. His response wasn't as important to me as the ability to talk to Him. I grew up believing that God was immanent, that He heard me when I spoke; and that was good enough for me. I talked to Him when I was happy and when I was sad, when I was excited and when I was scared. There wasn't a specific time or setting. I simply talked to Him whenever my heart desired.

I knew that God was all-powerful, too. So as a youngster, and with no real understanding about what this divine power meant, I would ask for His help in order to win my wrestling matches, that He would perhaps disable my opponents from countering my attacks. (My life in the sport of wrestling began the same year I became a Christian, so there has always been a special connection between the two for me). I would even ask that He sprinkle certain young ladies with loving feelings for me so that they would like me over the taller and much better looking boys. Ridiculous? Absolutely. But my relationship with God was real and all-consuming. It meant everything to me.

Now as an adult, my life experience has increased and I have even earned a degree in theology. The subject fascinates me! And even though I take issue with certain thoughts and expositions expressed by some theologians past and present, I can't help but believe that, while how we *think* about God is important, it does not necessarily trump how we *follow* Him. In other words, it is my fervent belief that God is after both the heart *and* the mind, but with the heart being a bit more of the goal. Or in order to avoid any dualism in separating the mind and the heart, it would be better said that God is after the whole being.

I think it's fair to say that fulfillment of theological inquiry is not a concern for most people. In fact, these debates are really only reflective of a small fraction of the Christian community. The majority of people are more concerned with *how to live*. They are more concerned with the practical side of understanding and relating to God. This is not to say that theology should be left to the experts. Everybody should engage in some sort of theological practice. After all, it's quite hard to follow someone or something if we do not first understand the person or thing we're intending to follow. But I fear the work of our role as Christians has been reversed for quite some time – the *thinking* has replaced the *following* in terms of which aspect is leading the bond. Without a doubt, a positive result of this recomposition includes centuries of profound theological thought and understanding. The negative, however, is that the infatuation with the 'thinking' has developed more schisms in the church than one could have possibly imagined. Some of these schisms, such as those which resulted from the historical church counsels, may have been necessary for the health and character of the church. But the truth is that many of them were not. They were, instead, a result of stubbornness and an emphasis on thought over praxis. And the same can be said for modern day church quarrels and divisions.

I admit that I have fallen into the aforementioned infatuation: belief in the superiority of the rational and theological mind. It's hard not to, especially when you engage the world of theological study and begin wrestling with the issues that have confronted the church. The truth is that when you engage this world, and in the course of developing your theology, you start to make your own declarations and judgments. Moreover, you begin to think that you see things clearer than anyone else has before, or that you are, at the very least, in a small group of enlightened thinkers. Too often I have seen the theological mind perform injustice on those who may not be as "well informed." I've been a part of this injustice. It takes humility to slap you in the face before you're brought back down to earth. God Himself did the "slapping" in order to help me see my stature with Him as an ignorant, little child looking up and trying to fathom the wonder of his heavenly Father.

The most interesting thing in all of this is that, as an adult, and as a former student of theology, I see more beauty in the faith of my six year old self than I do of my theologically astute self of today. My faith is stronger and more mature today, for sure; but there is something profoundly beautiful about my followership of God as a little boy whose faith was untainted by the quarrels that human beings eventually embrace as adults – both in the world and in the church. There's something about the peacefulness in the relationship that can only be manifested when or if a person embraces the gospel as a child. There's something about the closeness in the relationship, like a deep friendship unrivaled by any other.

Most children of the faith, it seems, don't enjoy church. Perhaps it's because their closeness with God is so secure that they simply don't recognize the significance of being a part of a church community. And perhaps this is why "older" people of the faith *need* church; because the closeness with God that once was as a child has weakened. Life came in. The world came in. And the power of them needs to be combated by a *community* of faith-filled people. Or maybe they chose to engage the faith as an adult, and their step into faith brings with it all sorts of baggage and hurt that requires a community of believers to help overcome heavy burdens and to walk through life together as they chase after God.

    Maybe my faith as a child was unique. It might be the case that others cannot relate to it. Nevertheless, I feel that maybe, when all is said and done, God's work in me is supposed to bring me back to my child-like faith. It may not look exactly the same, but some form of it perhaps; a form in which my belief and dependence on Him is child-like but my character is mature and perfected. Jesus states in the Gospel of Matthew that we need to "become like little children" in order to "enter the kingdom of heaven." So I can't be too far off from the truth. And if there is even a *hint* of truth to this suggestion, I can't help but yearn for it.

    All of this relates to the focus of this book. There's a sense in which the church needs to take a step back and rediscover the faith of a child, which, I will argue throughout the course of this book, corresponds to the humility inherent in the "faith of a wrestler." When we do this, not only do we return to the core of our faith but our communication of the gospel to others starts to become more authentic and transparent.

---

Despite the media interest in Christianity versus atheism (or the closely related agnosticism) as well as the many books written on the topic, it needs to be said: atheism is not a legitimate challenge to the faith. It may certainly be the case that there is an intellectual battle taking place (and will continue to take place) in regard to trying to prove or disprove the existence of God and so forth; but regardless of the debate's existence, neither side is going to falter at any given point. The battle will continue, and both sides will walk away thinking they are the victor.

As alluded to already, although there is interest by a small fraction of people in debates of this nature (i.e., scholars, the theologically trained, and a minority of lay Christians and non-Christians), most Americans (perhaps even people as a whole from every part of the world) could care less about apologetics or the opinions of scholars. This is not to suggest that these debates are meaningless. To be sure, there is some definite value in them. For instance, from the Christian perspective, alongside the mystery of God is the belief that He entered into time, space and history through the person of Jesus Christ; and being able to provide support for such a claim is important. But in terms of connecting to the larger body of people, these debates are not going to make much of a connection, at least not in today's postmodern, American culture. Christian author, Donald Miller, writes: "Sooner or later you just figure out there are some guys who don't believe in God and they can prove He doesn't exist, and there are some other guys who do believe in God and they can prove He does exist, and the argument stopped being about God a long time ago and now it's about who is smarter, and honestly I don't care."[1] Though writing as a Christian, his sentiment (I think) speaks for many people, non-Christians included.

According to the Pew Research Center, of the 22.8 percent of Americans 'unaffiliated' with a religious faith in 2014, 15.8 percent consider themselves spiritual. This is an increase from 12.1 percent in 2007, and more than double the current percentage of atheists and agnostics combined which stands at around 7.1 percent.[2] If these statistics serve

---

[1] Donald Miller, *Blue Like Jazz: Nonreligious Thoughts on Christian Spirituality* (Nashville, TN: Thomas Nelson, 2002).
[2] Pew Research Center. "America's Changing Religious Landscape: Christians Decline Sharply as Share of Population; Unaffiliated and Other Faiths Continue to Grow," Last modified May 12, 2015. Obtained from http://byfaithonline.com/americas-changing-religious-landscape/.

as an accurate depiction of the spiritual landscape within American culture, it is imperative that the church connect with these 'spiritually open or seeking yet religiously indifferent individuals.' In order to do this, communication of the gospel message can no longer be reflective of the status quo. The church must challenge and perhaps reconsider how it is communicating this message. In short, how do we communicate with the 15.8 percent in a way that helps the gospel message come to life?

The battle is not necessarily for the atheist who doesn't care about spiritual matters; the battle concerns the large percentage of people who contain some sort of belief in spirituality but who lack any interest in the Christian faith. These people are consumed in their day-to-day lives and have little or no interest at all in listening to advocates of the faith present philosophical or scientific arguments for the existence of God or rationale for specific Christian doctrines. When it comes down to it, they're just not interested. The real issue then is not atheism but a lack of genuine fervor. In other words, the main focus and challenge of the Christian faith in today's American culture is not necessarily turning atheists (and agnostics) into believers. The main focus and challenge is engaging the much, much larger percentage of people who are open to spirituality but who have no interest in the Christian faith. These people are not necessarily looking for something to grab their intellect (like the 7%); they're looking for something to stir excitement and truth within their hearts.

In fact, it could be argued that even the atheists are not looking for intellectual fulfillment. Just like everyone else, they are complex human beings with several other factors impacting their belief system. They, too, despite their arguments otherwise, are also looking for something to stir excitement and truth within their hearts. The problem, of course, is that many people who associate with an atheistic view of the world contain stronger resistance to even engaging matters of spirituality apart from trying to convince the other person that spiritual matters are nonsense.

I heard a pastor once suggest that this is most likely what Jesus meant when He said, "Do not give dogs what is sacred; do not throw your pearls to pigs. If you do, they may trample them under their feet, and turn and tear you to pieces" (Matthew 7:6). That is, the gospel is a pearl. It's the most beautiful treasure in this life. But there are some people who are simply intent on returning hatred in response to any proclamation of the gospel message. And while it is certainly possible that God can break through the resistant hearts of die-hard atheists (and has done so), the gospel is nevertheless more readily available to those who are actually seeking or who are at least open to spirituality. And so it should be no surprise that Jesus follows up in the very next verse by saying, "Ask and it will be given to you; seek and you will find; knock and the door will be opened to you" (Matthew 7:7). The gospel is available to such as these.

If this is true, how is the church supposed to make a connection? How are we, as Christians, supposed to connect with people who don't believe there is a *need* to discover a connection in the first place? How do we talk about the faith with those who, though open to spirituality, simply have no interest in discussing philosophical and theological matters or whose view of Christianity has been tainted by caricatures and misconceptions? The answer is that we (as believers) need to first rediscover the gospel ourselves. We need to get back to the heart of our faith, which I argue is discovered in the faith of a wrestler. This means ridding ourselves of strictly thinking in methods of intellectualism, certainties, and doctrine. We don't have all the answers and shouldn't pretend that we do. We're putting our trust in *the* answer: Jesus Christ. "The faith that God's people are called to embrace is one that encourages people to wrestle with God, to not be afraid of questions, and to act faithfully in the face of uncertainty."[3] Once we embrace the faith of a wrestler, then we can have genuine dialogue with others and let the Holy Spirit do His work.

True, we can't *force* people to be interested. But we can *encourage* and *enliven* interest. And, again, we can do so by rediscovering the foundation of our faith, putting away the idea that we have an answer to everything, and actively engaging others through their own available avenues. That is, by meeting people where they're at,

---

[3] Gregory A. Boyd, *Benefit of the Doubt: Breaking the Idol of Certainty*, (Grand Rapids, MI: Baker Book, 2013).

honing in on what *they* care about, and trying to utilize the 'points of contact' *they* provide. We can more effectively connect with them by approaching them as human beings rather than merely walking, talking minds. The faith of wrestler is the very approach that both brings us back to authentic Christian faith and allows us to engage the spiritually lost with a genuineness that connects faith to the real matters of life.

There was a time, perhaps, when well thought out responses to philosophical and theological inquiries was the route to take in trying to convince people that Christ truly is Messiah King – the very face of God and the proof of His pursuit of us. But this is, for the most part, no longer the case. The argument is not whether it *should* be. Personally, I am much more drawn to deep philosophical and theological discussions. This doesn't make me necessarily superior or even more authentic than those who could care less about discussions of this nature. On the contrary, it simply means that the culture has shifted; or maybe the culture has been this way for quite some time and we're just now noticing. Whatever the case may be, it's time to take seriously what the majority of people in our culture might be telling us. For me, it's not about conforming them to think as I do. I would much rather listen to them, engage them, and help guide them along a path which leads to the cross.

It is my belief, and the belief of most Christians, that the Christian faith is the answer to any individual's spirituality. By overlooking Christianity, or any other religious faith for that matter, and choosing to stand within their own category of spirituality, they are creating a religion of their own. Now, Christianity was never meant to bolster a religion per se, but it was meant to deliver truth about God and about ourselves. It was meant to reveal truth as only God knows it. Christianity is an invitation to say "yes" to God and partake in the truth that has been revealed:

> ...the message of Christ was not the introduction of a religion, but an introduction to truth about reality as God alone knows it. To deny Jesus' message while pursuing spirituality is to conjure an imaginary religion in an attempt to see heaven while sight is confined to the earth. That is precisely what Jesus challenged when he said, "I have come that [you] may have life" (John 10:10). His life spells living. Your life or my life, apart from Him, spells death.[4]

---

[4] Ravi Zacharias, *Jesus among Other Gods: The Absolute Claims of the Christian Message* (Nashville, TN: W Publishing Group, 2002).

# THEY'RE JUST NOT INTERESTED

# CHAPTER 1

# STILL DEALING WITH THE ENLIGHTENMENT

There's simply no way around it: winters in Minnesota are terrible. They're cold, snowy and way too long (some have lasted until early May). It was during such a winter that I was invited by a group of friends to attend a debate taking place on the University of Minnesota campus. It was a Christian versus atheist debate, and the topic (unsurprisingly): Does God Exist?

I had never been to a debate before. I wasn't sure what to expect; but as a Christian who was starting to find interest in intellectual discourse and who, quite frankly, had nothing better to do, I went.

My friends were students at the university, so the plan was to meet them at their dorm room. But of course it takes half a night to find a parking spot on the U of M campus, and this particular night was no different. After overcoming a bit of frustration in finding a place to park my car, I met up with my friends and we made the long walk across campus where the debate would be held.

The debate location was in one of the large lecture halls. But even as particularly large as the room was for college lectures, it probably wasn't the best fit for a debate of this type. Lots of people showed up and there were not enough seats to accommodate. So while my friends and I were able to frantically find available seats, a number of people had to stand in the back or sit on the floor along the aisle which ran down the middle of the room.

I wasn't familiar with either speaker. However, I quickly discovered that both of them embodied a confidence in their position that would make for an interesting encounter and a little bit of discomfort as well. The debate started off cordial. Each speaker had a chance to present his case in an opening statement, and the room was rather quiet as the audience listened. It wasn't until the rebuttal portion of the debate that things took a bit of a turn. For some reason or another, the audience came alive. So much so that I felt like I was attending a sporting event rather than an intellectual debate. And it was easy to discover who in the audience was in support of whom as cheers and hollers came forth after a rebuttal or snarky comment delivered by either speaker.

As the two speakers went back and forth, and the cheers and hollers continued to erupt from the audience, I quickly realized that the debate was not going to prove successful in changing anybody's mind either way. And it was the atheist's comment that really stuck with me. Looking and pointing at his Christian opponent, he said, "You can debate me all you want about science, history and philosophy, but you will never convince me that an all-loving God exists in the same world as cancer."

It didn't occur to me right away but it did plant a seed of something really important, something I would consider more fully later on. And that is, perhaps *information* doesn't necessarily lead to *transformation*. In other words, maybe we can engage one another intellectually all day long, but in the end, intellect is not the issue – at least not for most people.

I had mentioned previously that atheism is not a legitimate challenge to the Christian faith. And when it comes to considering life, along with the many questions about what this life means and our immediate role in it, I wholeheartedly stand by this assertion. Atheism simply doesn't offer anything in the realm of meaning and purpose. And these questions regarding meaning and purpose aren't necessarily deeply philosophical so much as they are deeply practical. Of course there are many philosophical tangents that can be taken relative to the meaning of life, but the reality is that meaning and purpose connect more on a personal level for people as opposed to philosophical speculation.

With that said, I reference this particular story because the atheist speaker's comment corresponds to the most common issue relative to the nonbeliever's struggle with embracing the Christian gospel: "the problem of evil (suffering)." That is, why is there so much evil and suffering in the world? And given that evil and suffering exist, doesn't that, by default, work against the notion that an all-good, all-loving God exists?

There are plenty of well-developed and convincing philosophical arguments that show how God exists alongside the existence of evil and suffering, and furthermore how the gospel is the answer to all of it. But the truth of the matter is the problem of evil is not an *intellectual* problem; it's a *personal* problem. It's a problem which connects to the very heart of every human being who has experienced it. Religious skeptic, Bart Ehrman, puts it this way:

> The problem of suffering became for me the problem of faith. After many years of grappling with the problem, trying to explain it, thinking through explanations that others have offered – some of them pat answers charming for simplicity, others highly sophisticated and nuanced reflections of serious philosophers and theologians – after thinking about the alleged answers and continuing to wrestle with the problem...I finally admitted defeat, came to realize that I could no longer believe in the God of my tradition, and acknowledged

that I was agnostic: I don't "know" if there is a God; but if there is one, he certainly isn't the one proclaimed by the Judeo-Christian tradition, the one who is actively and powerfully involved in this world.[5]

The greatest philosophical explanation in the world is not going to make evil and suffering any more tolerable. In short, philosophy doesn't cure cancer. Or to put it differently, while a solid argument may help a person *think* differently, it's not necessarily going to make him or her *feel* differently. Right *thinking* does not inevitably cause *belief*. The truth is that their loved one is still dead, or their life is still in shambles; and no matter what you say, he or she still feels the terrible anguish and heartache of their suffering. All we can confidently say is this: Jesus doesn't necessarily give an explanation for the pain and sorrow of the world. He comes and takes the pain upon Himself. Jesus doesn't explain why there is suffering, illness and death. He brings healing and hope. He allows evil to do its worst to Him, He exhausts it, drains it of its power and emerges with new life. God, through the person of Jesus Christ, *meets us in our suffering*. He faced it head on in His life, experienced the weight of it on the cross and conquered it in His resurrection. *This* is the God we believe in. Our *belief* is that, when we embrace Him, we are given the opportunity to experience, in part, the new life that He offers. And our *hope* is that, upon our mission in this life to

---
[5] Bart Ehrman, *God's Problem: How the Bible Fails to Answer Our Most Important Question – Why We* Suffer (New York: HarperOne, 2009).

bring heaven to earth, to bring God's goodness and love to our broken world, we will transition into eternity with Him and experience the *fullness* of this new life. Yes, we as a community of Christian believers have (at times) been failures in this mission. Sometimes we have allowed ourselves to be blinded by other things and unfortunately contributed to some of the pain in this world. But this does not dismiss the truth of the mission itself.

It took a while to really sink in, but sometime after the debate I started to question the Christian approach. Are we really going about this the right way? Are we really trying to win lives for the gospel or are we more concerned with sounding rational? Are we actually connecting with people and wrestling with their uncertainties, or are we still dealing with an intellectual movement that charged with force into the world centuries ago?

## *The Enlightenment*

The Age of the Enlightenment was an era dating back to about the seventeenth century. It was a movement in which cultural and intellectual forces in Western Europe emphasized reason, analysis and individualism as opposed to the traditional lines of authority such as God and religion. As hard as it might be for some people to acknowledge, God and religion have been central to philosophy, culture and society since the dawn of history. So this shift in thought and life was a significant one.

This movement especially created a significant challenge for the religious thinkers of the time. Challenges to the faith were taking a new form – that is, being able to maintain relevance within the confines of new philosophical ideas. It's not that Christianity hadn't faced a similar challenge with Greek philosophy centuries before. But the thoughts and expositions weren't necessarily repackaged Greek philosophical categories. Some of it was in fact new. For instance, whereas much of Greek philosophy took the divine (or God) for granted as part of the groundwork and starting point of its thought, Enlightenment philosophy did not. The groundwork and starting point of Enlightenment thought was the individual human being. In other words, all philosophical speculation on matters of life started with the independent, freethinking individual. As a result, the authority of the church in social, cultural and political life was questioned.

While this movement started in Europe, it expanded across the rest of the Western world (i.e., America). And to a certain degree, the Western world has never quite moved past it. Religious thinkers have been presenting their theology with the Enlightenment's influence in the background ever since. Just consider the number of Christian apologists today who are deep in the practice of speaking and writing about the "reasonableness of Christianity." As mentioned before, there is arguably a place for this. However, the church's engagement with this mode of thinking is evidence of how much the

Enlightenment continues to impact us. Renowned theologian, Alister McGrath, offers a serious assessment of evangelical Christianity and its continued wrestling with the Enlightenment: "Certain central Enlightenment ideas appear to have been uncritically taken on board by some evangelicals, with the result that part of the movement runs the risk of becoming secret prisoner of a secular outlook which is now dying before our eyes."[6]

While respecting the fact that there were several influential thinkers of the Enlightenment and that it was a relatively complex period in time, there were a few thinkers in particular who had a considerable impact on Western thought: Rene' Descartes, John Locke and Immanuel Kant. These philosophers were leaders, each in their own right, in terms of proposing that knowledge is based on self-evident truths of reason or evidences of the senses. In other words, knowledge and truth must have a connection to rational thought and/or we must be able to see, touch, or feel it. It was a way of thinking obsessed with rational certainty and tended to rule out of bounds any truth claims based on faith and revelation. Simply put, only the practice of reason was believed to be capable of obtaining real knowledge and truth. Experience, on the other hand, was deemed altogether subjective and therefore unable to lead to knowledge, let alone truth. You may recall Descartes' famous line, "I think, therefore I

---

[6] Alister McGrath, *A Passion for Truth: The Intellectual Coherence of Evangelicalism* (Downers Grove, IL: InterVarsity, 1996).

am;"[7] a proposition which became a foundational element of Western philosophy as it was believed to form a basis for all knowledge (as described above). In short, knowledge and subsequent belief is gained through the act of thinking. In fact, it is the act of thinking which proves our very existence.

Lesslie Newbigin, a great Christian leader of the latter half of the twentieth century, suggested that the influence of Descartes, in particular, created a false dualism in the method of knowing. That is, Descartes separated the mind from the body, as if the mind is a detached entity from the rest of the human body in terms of gaining knowledge and truth, as if the mind is the sole "driver" of the body. Newbigin maintained that this dualism is wrong. In other words, we don't know things or establish belief in something simply by intellectual assent. We know things and establish belief as a result of a personal commitment to knowing – it's an act which requires the whole person. We are not merely (or even primarily) rational beings. We are also beings of emotion, conscience, spirit and will. All of these aspects are involved in the process of gaining knowledge and truth, and establishing belief.

However, even if we were to just consider the human mind, any individual – scientist, historian,

---

[7] Rene' *Descartes, Discourse on the Method of Rightly Conducting the Reason, and Seeking Truth in the Sciences* (1637).

philosopher or "average Joe" – makes a decision to put their trust in the information provided by thinkers and contributors of the past as well as the information provided by thinkers and contributors of the present; not to mention the impact of time, circumstance and culture in the process of personal interpretation. And whatever he or she concludes from this information and interpretation (as well as the learned 'tradition' of interpretation) is nothing short of a commitment.

But again, we do not merely progress *intellectually; we step into a commitment of knowledge and truth with our whole being*. Another way of putting this is that the journey of knowledge and truth (and belief) is not one that is merely psychologically driven. Furthermore, truth is not something out there for the taking, something to possess; truth is something to experience.

## *Experience versus Intellect*

All of this leads to the matter of knowledge and truth as it pertains to the Christian faith. And this is the most important aspect in this discussion as believers and communicators of God's message (His gospel) to the world. When we claim knowledge, we are claiming *personal* knowledge, in that we have encountered a *person* (Jesus Christ) and have put our trust in Him. And when we claim truth, we are claiming to have encountered *Truth incarnate*: Jesus Christ. In other words, we are claiming to have encountered the Truth by which all other truths discover their reference point.

In short, the gospel is a personal calling which requires a personal response. Jesus did not acquire disciples by way of rational certainties. He did not offer arguments based on logic and reason. He offered Himself and then simply declared, "Follow me." As Newbigin describes it, "Christian faith is not a matter of logically demonstrable certainties but of the total commitment of fallible human beings putting their trust in the faithful God who has called them."[8]

Corresponding to this, there has been a notable struggle within the Christian faith that predates the Enlightenment but which was nevertheless accentuated by it. That is, the balance between *experience* and *intellect*. The Pietist movement of the late seventeenth century and into the nineteenth century, for instance, was a movement in Christianity which attempted to get back to the *spiritual experience* of the faith. However, with such a strong emphasis on intellectualism, both in the past as well as in the present, the thrust for reason has often dismissed piety (experience) as a central component. Simply put, while it is suggested that Christians should take seriously the

---

[8] Lesslie Newbigin, *Proper Confidence: Faith, Doubt, and Certainty in Christian Discipleship*, (Grand Rapids, MI: Wm. B. Eerdmans Publishing, 1995).

opportunity to experience God and His love, the suggestion seems to be of secondary value. Christian leaders and scholars (especially conservatives) have been in the business of sustaining Christian *doctrine* as the foremost objective through the process of rational certainty or similar methods. In other words, it is believed that Christians must *think correctly* before they can authentically experience God. As a result, there has been this tension between piety (experience) and reason (intellect and/or doctrine). And as Christian leaders and scholars exercise this emphasis on reason, it trickles down to the large body of lay Christians who in turn actively or subconsciously repeat whatever it is they have heard. Even though the following quote specifically accuses Christianity of the conservative type, it's important to recognize that liberal Christianity has been equally affected by the Enlightenment, just in different ways. That is, while conservative, evangelical Christianity has embraced Enlightenment thought as a means to sustain and give reason for traditional beliefs, liberal Christianity has embraced Enlightenment thought as a means to make an old religion relevant to the ever changing times.

> …traditional, conservative evangelical theology is by and large captivated by a modern quest for rational certainty that is living off the dregs of Enlightenment foundationalism if not explicitly working with it. The problem is that such indubitable foundations yielding rational certainty are nowhere to be found in the

postmodern world; we now know that all knowledge arises within and hangs on beliefs shaped by perspectives shared by communities created by stories and traditions. Also, such rationalistic epistemology is basically unbiblical and sub-Christian. It ignores the roles of sin and the Holy Spirit and faith in knowing truth Christianly.[9]

This impact of Enlightenment thought and the noted emphasis to 'think correctly,' reminds me of a story I heard from a good friend.

## Tension in a Christian Book Study

Something I have tried to make a habit of doing for a number of years now is schedule time to meet one-on-one with friends. Life can get busy with work, family, holidays and special events; and amidst the chaotic nature of life, it's easy to forget about sustaining and growing genuine friendships. But these relationships are important to me, so I do what I can to make sure I'm intentional about connecting somewhat consistently with those whom I consider friends. I scheduled to get together with Derek weeks in advance, and after a long day at work, I was ready to head to the coffee shop, sit back, relax and talk.

---

[9] Roger E. Olson, *Reformed and Always Reforming: The Postconservative Approach to Evangelical Theology* (Grand Rapids, MI: Baker Academic, 2007).

Derek has a knack for being on time, which I appreciate. So it was no surprise to see him already sitting there when I walked into the doors of the coffee shop, and with a chair right next to him waiting for me. We exchanged hugs, grabbed our coffees and started talking.

Derek, only a few months back, had started going to the same church as me. And I remembered that he was taking one of the Wednesday evening classes available called "Reason for God," based off the Tim Keller book of the same title. So I asked him how it was going. He told me that the class had actually concluded the previous week, and the most excitement in the class took place in the final meeting. Two of the participants in the class created a considerable amount of tension within their interaction about the Bible and the creation story in the book of Genesis.

The interaction involved a middle-aged woman (teacher) and a middle-aged man (chemist). In discussing the section in Keller's book pertaining to science and creation, the man admitted to the group that he did not believe in a literal account of the creation story and stated that he believed the earth to be over ten billion years old. The woman was appalled by this, and called the man's faith into question. "If you think the earth is over ten billion years old, how can you say that you believe the Bible? How can you be a Christian?"

The man very kindly tried to explain himself, but every explanation he gave was quickly followed up with another accusation by the passionate and concerned woman. After several instances of back-and-forth, the man finally had enough and said, "Look, I believe in Jesus Christ, and so do you. I believe that he was God in the flesh, died on the cross for my sins, and rose again from the dead giving hope and salvation to all who believe in him. So do you. We have common ground in this. All the rest is stuff that we can discuss. We can talk about it. But a literal interpretation of the biblical creation story is not what contains my hope and salvation. Jesus, and Jesus alone, contains this."

This is just a brief example of the difficulties that take place within our Christian community when we adopt an inflexible, staunch mode of thinking, one in which our thinking on certain matters takes precedence over our heart. Or to put it differently, when our thinking about certain aspects of Christianity take precedence over the very foundation of our faith, which is Jesus Himself.

I heard a well-known scholar discuss something similar when he talked about what he referred to as the "house-of-cards faith" of many Christians. A house of cards is a constructive piece created by stacking and placing playing cards in a creative way in order to make a "house." They're very fragile, and removing any single card causes the entire structure to fall apart. This scholar suggested that the Christian faith of a number of people can be described in a similar way as it pertains to their perspective on the Bible and what it says, as well as their overall theology.

So each card represents personal beliefs on the Bible and certain doctrines or theological opinions. They build their faith on these, and each card is interconnected to the point that, if any single piece (or belief) is proven to be false, then their entire faith comes crumbling down. What many of these Christians come to find is that their house-of-cards faith is very unstable. They either end up disappointed, or at the very least, overly paranoid about disrupting any single held belief in fear that their Christian faith is on the line. The problem of course is that these Christians are not putting the foundation of their faith in Jesus Christ, but instead on personally held beliefs about the Bible and doctrine. They essentially have a relationship with their *beliefs* rather than a relationship with Jesus Christ.

This impacts our communication to those outside the Christian community as well. Nonbelievers have no interest in listening to, let alone engaging, arguments about this or that element of the Bible or theology. It only encourages the idea that Christians are less concerned about real life and authentically engaging people with the gospel, and more concerned about being right when it comes to biblical and theological disputes. Nonbelievers may faintly hear some notion about relationship with Christ as the foundation of Christianity, but what they actually see tells a different story. What they actually see, and hear more prominently, involves religious jargon that they don't understand.

The man in the above story is correct. Proper perspective in regard to our faith as Christians should be centered on Jesus Christ (His life, death and resurrection), the salvation and hope that He brings, as well as the transformation of our lives in relationship with Him. Christianity is not about who is in and who is out; it's about authentic discipleship of Jesus Christ. Different opinions on aspects of the Bible are going to exist in our community. What's important is not that we agree on every single detail. What's important is that we agree on the most important detail: Jesus Christ. What's important is that we recognize the Bible as vitally important in knowing God more and allowing Him to shape our lives. What's important is not that we all agree on a literal six days of creation, for example. What's important is that we all agree we can encounter the living God within the pages of the Bible. Quite frankly, the Bible is not a book of science or philosophy! It's God's story! It's a depiction of God's dynamic relationship with His people, and a depiction which is illustrated by the use of different types of literature – poetry, wisdom literature, gospels, epistles, apocalyptic literature, and so forth. Each type of literature utilizes a different method with which to deliver God's message or to communicate God's dealings with the world. This is important to acknowledge if we are to move forward as a community of believers.

## *Moving Past the Enlightenment*

This chapter revealed something very important. That is, the impact of the Enlightenment is real and pervasive. We need to figure out a way in which to move past it, not just for the sake of deepening our own faith but for the sake of communicating better to others about what the Christian faith actually is and what it is offering. What's interesting is that the majority of Christians have no clue that they have been impacted by this movement, in that they don't see their faith as particularly intellectual or centered on their thinking. They hold true to their faith and what they have learned from their pastors regarding the necessities and doctrines of authentic Christian faith. But what has happened is that they've turned the word of their pastors, and the Bible, into a bedrock of certainties, not much different than the way intellectuals have turned the word of philosophers and scientists into their own bedrock of certainties. What's worse is that Christians have put their pastors' particular *interpretation* of the Bible on a pedestal above Christ Himself!

Does the Bible reveal truth? Absolutely! But it's not discussing the truth(s) of certainty; it's discussing the truth of God and His dealings with the world. It's discussing His grand story of redemption which is culminated in the person of Jesus Christ. It's a story in which each and every one of us, as believers in Jesus, can actually find ourselves in it! God's story becomes our story! What's more is that the Bible does not encapsulate God. God is greater than the Bible and our interpretations of it!

When you get down to it, the issue described above leads to an ugly word: legalism. Instead of the Christian faith representing the uniqueness of divine love and grace, we turn it into a legalistic system no different than that of other religions. This is, in part, what Jesus passionately fought against whenever confronted by the Pharisees (the Jewish leaders of the time). The Pharisees were relentless in accusing Jesus of not following the religious rules and traditions of scripture. In fact, it could be suggested that they accused Jesus of bad theology and a blatant dismissiveness toward doctrine. In response, Jesus accused them of using the scriptures and Jewish religious law (and doctrine) as a god; or at the very least resources with which to gain spiritual life. In fact, He suggested that they allowed the scriptures, for example, and their interpretations of it, to distract them from seeing the very person the scriptures speak of, the very source of true life: Him. "You study the Scriptures diligently because you think that in them you have eternal life. These are the very scriptures that testify about me, yet you refuse to come to me to have life" (John 5:39-40).

And remember the response of Jesus toward the Pharisees regarding following laws of Jewish religion? He said, "'Love the Lord your God with all your heart and with all your soul and with all your mind.' This is the first and greatest commandment. And the second is like it: 'Love your neighbor as yourself.' All the Law and the Prophets hang on these two commandments" (Matthew 22:37-40). Simply put, *love* is part and parcel to the Law of God. If love is missing, the Law is useless. The Scriptures and Jewish Law were never meant as resources of self-righteousness, legalism, or fulfillment of spiritual life, which many of the Pharisees had made them out to be. The Scriptures and Jewish Law were meant to serve as a guideline for individuals whose sole desire in following them was out of love for God and emulating His goodness.

Apart from this, I think the influence of the Enlightenment is pretty apparent as it regards many contemporary Christian leaders and scholars. Intellectualism, psychologically-driven belief, or an emphasis on how a person *thinks* about God, has taken precedence over the importance of a transformed life. Despite some disagreements leveled at theologian, Clark Pinnock, while he was still living, I wholeheartedly agree with his sentiment when he wrote, "It is high time we became less preoccupied with rational certainty and doctrinal precision and more concerned with telling the

Christian story with its rich interplay of meanings that speak to all our human needs."[10]

Before we get to my proposal for a more authentic approach to the Christian faith, we need to address some pushback that exists in resisting and moving past the impact of the Enlightenment.

---

[10] Clark Pinnock, *Tracking the Maze: Finding Our Way through Modern Theology from an Evangelical Perspective* (San Francisco, CA: Harper & Row, 1990).

# THEY'RE JUST NOT INTERESTED

# CHAPTER 2

# THE CROSS IS FOOLISHNESS

In advocating for a move away from the rationalism (the intellectualism), the emphasis on the mind apparent in Enlightenment thought, there is definitely some pushback; and this chapter will highlight a very important element relative to this. I will begin with a statement made by my older brother when I was in conversation with him.

I had made a comment regarding something to the extent that, as much as I love engaging in intellectual debate, I think it's important to acknowledge that Jesus did not acquire disciples by way of rational certainties. Instead, He merely offered Himself. I continued by saying that I don't believe the mind to be the sole driver of the body when it comes to putting our belief in something, and that *belief* involves the entire person, that it is composed of many influencing factors and is enacted by the will.

"I'm not sure I follow what you just said, Mike," he said. "Thinking requires intellect, but believing requires something besides intellect? I'm also not sure I accept your premise. Jesus did demonstrate superior wisdom and knowledge of scripture. He also walked around for three years healing the sick, raising the dead, and feeding people by the thousands. I can't think of acts which more clearly demonstrated a supernatural authority over this world."

To be honest, I was happy to hear my brother responding this way. He was a late comer to the faith despite being exposed to it all his life, and his response showed that he really cares about this stuff and has taken the time to familiarize himself with the Bible. In fact, I've been inspired by some of his thoughts regarding the Christian life. I really admire him. However, he made a significant mistake in his line of thinking, and the remainder of this chapter will serve as a response to my brother's statement and challenge.

## *Knowledge versus Wisdom*

As described in the previous chapter, when I talk about knowledge and certainty, I am specifically referring to knowledge based on reason and as championed by the Enlightenment. This is also known as "epistemological" knowledge. And this was somewhat foreign to the Bible. Yet as modern human beings we rely heavily upon it. Also, there's a big difference between knowledge and wisdom. A person can be very knowledgeable but nevertheless not wise. Or as a somewhat simple example, a person with a Ph.D. at the end of their name contains superior knowledge, but that does not necessarily mean he or she is superior in wisdom. Wisdom (unlike knowledge) contains important and practical insight to living a good life, or from a Christian perspective, a God-centered life. Knowledge and wisdom are not one and the same.

There's another important distinction here: rational knowledge (epistemology) is not the same as knowledge of scripture. It is true that Jesus was incredibly knowledgeable of scripture and also wise. In fact, He was so wise that He stood out as such to those whom He interacted with. And that's important here, because it wasn't his intellectual prowess that garnered the attention of others; it was His outstanding wisdom, a wisdom which could only be obtained from knowledge of scripture (not rational knowledge).

Furthermore, Jesus spoke with *authority*, which garnered even more attention! Jesus was providing His own interpretation of scripture as well as adding to it (i.e., "You've heard it said...But I [Jesus] say..."). This was completely unheard of! You see, Jewish teachers (like the Pharisees) would speak with the authority of scripture as well as the authority of past teachers of Jewish law. In other words, they would merely read scripture and communicate its interpretation based on tradition. But Jesus didn't do this. *Jesus ascribed authority to Himself*! He provided His own interpretations, He added on to scripture, and He also referred to Himself as the very *fulfillment* of scripture! After reading from the book of Isaiah in its description of the coming Messiah, He says (referring to Himself), "Today, this scripture is fulfilled in your hearing" (Luke 4:21).

## *A Lesson from Paul in 1 Corinthians*

I've been involved in a men's Bible study for a couple of years now. We meet at a coffee shop once a month on Saturday mornings. One particular meeting we were working through the book of 1 Corinthians. And right away in the opening chapter includes the discussion of knowledge and the wisdom of this world compared with the gospel of Jesus Christ. Paul states that the message of the cross is "foolishness" to the world. He writes, "For the message of the cross is foolishness to those who are perishing, but to us who are being saved it is the power of God" (1 Corinthians 1:18). He goes on to develop a contrast between the contemporary philosophy of the time with that of the gospel. Simply put, the gospel is not meant to appease the philosophically minded. And it's interesting because, in this letter of Paul's, we discover that the early church was already dealing with the difficulty of being thought of by others as essentially ignorant and stupid. The City of Corinth may have not been Athens, but it was nevertheless still a hub of philosophy. What's more is that the majority of the church in Corinth were gentiles (not Jewish). They were converts from this very city of intellectuals. Therefore, they were already trying to make their faith fit into the philosophy of the time. I've argued in this book that we are still to this day dealing with this issue. However, as the scriptures indicate, this wasn't just an issue brought about through the Enlightenment; the issue began as far back as the early stages of the Christian church. In short, we have always struggled with trying to present ourselves and our faith as reasonable.

Here's an important point to consider: Prior to the Enlightenment, God was taken for granted. That is, it was assumed that a greater being of some kind existed. And this wasn't necessarily the result of extensive intellectual processes. Belief in the existence of God simply made sense. Also, it's fair to say that, while God as Creator may very well be discovered through the likes of reason, *the message of the cross cannot*. Think about it. We (as Christians) are not just talking about belief in a Creator God. We are not merely proclaiming God's existence. The existence of God wasn't really a question back in the early church, and has only garnered questioning in modern times. We are proclaiming something far more profound. We are proclaiming that God has invited all of humanity into relationship with Him through the person of Jesus Christ! And therefore, as devoted Christians, we are proclaiming to have a relationship with a man who died two thousand years ago, but who was resurrected from the dead. We are proclaiming that He brought salvation to the world to those who believe in Him, and lives in us through the power of the Holy Spirit. This is not rational! Yet we know it to be the truth.

## *Proper Confidence*

Lesslie Newbigin, who was mentioned in the first chapter, offers an alternative perspective relative to the hope and assuredness we experience in Christ Jesus, and as revealed through our Christian faith. Newbigin states that a more appropriate explanation of the knowledge, certainty, and belief we experience in Christ is "proper confidence." Proper confidence is more aligned with the type of confidence and faith we have in Christ, and it has nothing to do with certainty of the rational type as espoused in Enlightenment thought. It's *relational* knowledge. Proper confidence is biblical certainty and reflective of the faith of a wrestler. It's the type of faith that the book of Hebrews describes when it reads, "Now faith is confidence in what we hope for and assurance about what we do not see" (Hebrews 11:1). It's a matter of trust. It's trusting that God will redeem us and His creation. It's putting trust in God's faithfulness and the promise that His son, Jesus, truly brought salvation to the world and will carry out this salvation to completion. And this confidence is not merely a product of human effort, either. On the contrary, God has provided us a 'helper' and advocate: His Holy Spirit. The Spirit of God aids us through life; and when we rely on Him, His Spirit enlivens our confidence and trust in Him. The Spirit bears witness to Jesus Christ and what He did for us (2 Corinthians 5:5-8). What's more is that the Bible also bears witness to Him (though on a secondary level to that of the Spirit). Therefore, we can be confident ("properly confident") that Christ – His life, death, resurrection, and the unmerited grace and salvation discovered through Him – is worthy of our faith and trust.

I think the following story might help put all of this into perspective.

## *The Gospel of Atheism*

When I was a young twenty-something, I attended a church which included authentic participation with the surrounding community as part of its mission. The purpose was not simply to exist as a religious group but to be actively involved in the community.

Let me be clear that we were not walking around, knocking on people's doors or handing out bibles. Instead, we were encouraged to simply engage in conversation with others: listen to them, get to know them. If they brought up questions about God, great; if they didn't, that was fine, too. Additionally, the church would host social events and invite everyone in the community to join.

There is one encounter in particular that has always stuck with me, and more so in a peculiar and somewhat frustrating way. My friend Ben and I arrived at church that evening, only to discover that the service was cancelled due to another night out engaging with the community. Some people stuck around the area, while others (including Ben and I) decided to head downtown to Minneapolis, which was fairly close by. Ben is a pretty outgoing guy, so when we arrived we were welcomed into conversation with a small group of people rather easily (two guys and a girl). The conversation was light-hearted, and they seemed very kind.

We turned a corner on the sidewalk and left the busyness of the main area of the city behind us. It was now quiet, and the five of us stopped walking. Out of curiosity, and due to the fact that he was doing most of the talking, one of the guys asked us why we were so willing to enter into conversation with them. Ben and I explained who we were, and shared with him that we were part of a church that encouraged us to be intentional about connecting with others. The gentleman expressed that he really appreciated our effort, but then decided that it would be a great opportunity for him to set us straight on the whole issue of God and religion.

"I used to go to church," he said in a condescending tone, "but then I grew up."

Ben and I looked at each other a bit surprised by his statement, but allowed him to continue.

"You see, sooner or later, if you're honest with yourself, you realize that God doesn't really exist. He's a figment of our imagination in order to make life more tolerable. The world is a messed up place, and it makes us feel better knowing that maybe someone or something is in control of this whole mess we call life, that someone or something is going to someday make things better, or that there is a divine reason for our struggles." The gentleman paused for a moment and asked Ben directly, "Why is it that you believe in God? Why do you think you need him?"

"I believe what the Bible says about who Jesus was and is," Ben responded. "I believe that without God, life doesn't really make much sense. I believe that I am personally experiencing God's presence in my life. I don't believe in God because I need a crutch in life, if that's what you're suggesting."

"Okay, that's fine. I'm just saying that we as a human race need to kind of move past this whole God and religion thing. You don't need him. Everything you need is already there within yourself." As he said this he pointed his finger at Ben's chest. "I mean, you're a really great guy, Ben. You're kind, you're genuine…and that's because that stuff is already in you, man. You don't need God to be who you are. And you don't need religion to be who you are, either."

"With all due respect, I disagree with you," Ben said. "I'm telling you that God is not a crutch for me. He's real and alive. I experience Him…"

The gentleman cut him off, "Do me favor," he said. "The next time you pray, do a little experiment. First pray to God, and see what happens. And then pray to a gallon of milk, and see what happens. I guarantee you will receive the same results. Praying to God is like praying to a gallon of milk. Neither of them can do anything for you."

It was at this point I realized we were recipients of the gospel of atheism.

At that time in our lives, I don't think Ben or I were capable of dialoguing with this guy successfully. We were passionate about our faith, for sure; but we lacked the tools of knowledge and communication in order to combat his skepticism. Yet, at the same time, this gentleman affirmed the idea that many who ascribe to an atheistic worldview are only willing to engage spiritual dialogue as a means to express their belief that spiritual matters are nothing but nonsense.

But here's the thing that still frustrates me about this encounter: It's the suggestion that the atheist or the non-religious type is the "enlightened one," that they carry a message of intellectual freedom, of a release from the controlling grasp of an imaginary God. Or if the picture of God is not one of unwanted and unwarranted divine control, then it's a picture of God as a warm security blanket – a thing that really has no power to save at all, but the thought and feeling of it makes a person feel at ease. It's a position which centers the dialogue on methods of rational certainty; that Christians, for instance, are stuck in a mental prison of ignorance and immaturity. And if only we could free ourselves from this prison would we be able to realize that our highly evolved minds have moved past God and religion. And as the gospel of atheism espouses: real knowledge and truth is out there for the taking through the aid of science and reason. God is for children, not adults.

    Moreover, it frustrates me that it is suggested *belief* is a product of reason alone, as if human beings are merely rational animals, or that reason is the leader and controller of the human being despite influences of emotion, conscience, spirit, and will. As mentioned already, belief is something which includes the whole person. In other words, the human being is not just a functioning mind. It takes every unique and influential part of a human being in order to step into belief. The mind is an aid to belief, not the authority.

    The first part of this book has set the stage for my proposal. If we should move past a faith of certainties, then what should we replace it with? What type of faith is going to more authentically express our own? And what type of faith is going to allow us to better reach the 'spiritually open or seeking yet religiously indifferent?' It is my proposal that Christians should embrace the faith of a wrestler. And it's to this that we now turn.

## THEY'RE JUST NOT INTERESTED

# CHAPTER 3

# THE FAITH OF A WRESTLER

As I walked off the mat and into the arena tunnel at the 2003 Minnesota state tournament, I felt a sense of relief. You see, the brackets were not seeded. So as the #1 ranked wrestler in the state – with only one loss on my record coming from an Iowa wrestler earlier in the season – I faced the #3 ranked wrestler the very first round after he had been upset in the section tournament the week before. He was the only in-state opponent who had posed a significant challenge to me all year. It bothered me that we were meeting so soon in my quest for a state championship, but I accepted the situation for what it was and prepared for battle. After fighting off a barrage of strong underhooks, I scored the only takedown in the match toward the end of the third period, and came away with a 3-1 victory.

I sat in the tunnel, elated with moving past who I deemed to be my only worthy opponent. I hadn't won a state championship since my freshman year in Missouri before the move to Minnesota, and I expressed to my coaches that the hard work was essentially done. "That's it," I said. "The state championship is mine. He was the toughest guy I would face, and I put him away. I can coast to the finals now."

Both coaches looked at me, somewhat surprised. I wasn't normally the loud, confident type. "Well, he may have been your biggest threat," said coach Wellstone, looking into my eyes a bit concerned, "but you still need to prepare for your upcoming matches. Don't celebrate just yet."

"Yea, yea, I know. But you don't understand. I just put away the only guy who had a chance at stopping me from reaching the finals."

"I do understand, Mike." Wellstone put his arm around me. "Just stay focused, okay?"

The next round came up fast. I stepped on the mat with my unranked opponent and put my takedown skills on display. I took him down, let him up, took him down, let him up. I was racking up points and putting considerable distance between us. It wasn't until the third and final period that the momentum started to shift. I continued to take shots, but my opponent wasn't giving up so easily. He started to counter hard and ended up scoring a couple takedowns off my attacks. Confused about what was happening, and noticing that the score was closer than I thought, I pulled back from being offensive and went on the defense instead. My opponent must have seen the fear in my eyes, because he came at me like a starving lion. Earning a point for stalling, all he needed was a takedown to tie the match and send it into overtime. In the final seconds of the match, he hit a perfect ankle pick on the edge of the mat and secured the takedown.

    Neither of us showed any legitimate scoring opportunities in overtime, and so double-overtime was going to have to decide the match. I wasn't much of a "rider" as a junior (it wasn't until my senior year of high school that I developed a significant amount of skill and confidence in the top position); so I chose bottom, hoping I would get away rather easily and end this confusing nightmare. However, my opponent had a different plan in mind. He wasn't going to let me get away without a fight. Those thirty seconds in double-overtime were probably the longest of my life. Every scramble ended in a quick stalemate or out of bounds. I simply couldn't escape. I saw the final seconds fade away, and when it was over, I rested on the mat with my hands covering my face – embarrassed and dejected. I slowly got up and looked over at my coaches. A part of me hoped they would send some signal that this was all just a bad dream. But they didn't. It was very much real. I shook my opponent's hand and walked off the mat – sick to my stomach and caught in a state of shock.

This loss was such a painful blow to my life that I contemplated quitting the sport and forfeit competing the following year as a senior. I simply couldn't see any sense of redemption. The sport of wrestling had been a roller coaster of emotions for me. I put in a great deal of hard work, even felt confident that I would achieve state champion status, but in the end, I was confronted with an unexpected battle with an unexpected competitor, and lost. I had experienced an equally painful loss the year previous which kept me from the state finals. And despite returning the next season and having success all year, as revealed in the above story, I discovered heartbreaking disappointment at the one tournament that truly mattered.

After much reflection, I did decide to return for my senior campaign. And while the losses from the previous two seasons were in the back of my mind, I stayed focused and kept my eyes on the goal ahead. I made it to the state finals in convincing fashion, and finally repeated as state champion with a win in the championship match.

## *Faith and Wrestling*

The most revolutionary concept I have discovered when it comes to my own faith is that faith (of the Christian type) is not about growing in certainties; it's about the freedom to wrestle with God and all that He means and allowing Him to shape my life in the midst of this struggle. What's more is that (I believe) God, in a way, *desires* our wrestling with Him; because wrestling infers that we are taking Him seriously. Moreover, it allows for the greatest possibility of intimacy. Why? Because if we come out the other side of this wrestling match, and put our faith and trust in Him, it means that we have truly considered what a relationship with Him entails for our lives. A decision of faith in God following a time of wrestling with Him does not leave room for inauthenticity. It is wholly and completely authentic by its very nature.

What's more is that this wrestling continues even after a decision of faith has been made. The only difference is the purpose of the wrestling: the initial wrestling comes with the hope of faith being born, whereas once faith is born in the individual, the purpose is then to grow and deepen that faith.

This is in contrast to what has been discussed thus far in the book: rational certainty or a focus on the mind as it pertains to the Christian faith. The thinking within the faith of wrestler is untainted by Enlightenment thought.

When I think about the faith of a wrestler, I am envisioning both the act as well as the concept. I was involved in the sport of wrestling from the age of six and all the way into my early twenties. The ups and downs and the overall struggle that a wrestler goes through (as briefly revealed in the story I shared to open up this chapter) is a metaphor for life. Simply put, life is tough, life is filled with ups and downs, life is a wrestling match. And the same is true for faith.

I am also aware of the wrestling we must do when it comes to dealing with the fallenness of this world and the evil that is apparent. And we can't forget the story of Jacob wrestling with God in the book of Genesis which captures both the physical and conceptual nature of our wrestling with God in its story. In fact, in order to grasp the faith of a wrestler, the story of Jacob's wrestling match with God is necessary to uncover.

Readers who are familiar with my previous work may initially find the following section, as well as the subsequent chapter, to be somewhat of a review. However, I encourage them to press on. For the information has been expanded upon and will be very helpful in grasping the message within this book.

## *Jacob Wrestles with God*

Genesis chapter 32 is where we find this prolific story of Jacob. But before jumping into the story, it's important to note what took place prior to Jacob's wrestling match with God. That is, it comes after Jacob has stolen the birthright and blessing from his brother, Esau. And he steals the blessing, specifically, by pretending to be Esau and manipulating their father, Isaac, who was essentially legally blind due to old age. Jacob was asked twice by his father regarding his name, and both times Jacob responded that his name was Esau. In believing that it was truly Esau standing before him, he places the blessing upon Jacob.

Jacob is caught immediately afterwards and runs away in fear for his life. As a result, he has been gone for many years, is now married, has children, and now God is calling him back to his homeland to reconcile with his brother.

Genesis 32:24-31 reads: "So Jacob was left alone, and a man wrestled with him till daybreak. When the man saw that he could not overpower him, he touched the socket of Jacob's hip so that his hip was wrenched as he wrestled with the man. Then the man said, 'Let me go, for it is daybreak.'

But Jacob replied, 'I will not let you go unless you bless me.'

The man asked him, 'What is your name?'

'Jacob,' he answered.

Then the man said, 'Your name will no longer be Jacob, but Israel, because you have struggled with God and with humans and have overcome.'

Jacob said, 'Please tell me your name.'

But he replied, 'Why do you ask my name?' Then he blessed him there.

So Jacob called the place Peniel, saying, 'It is because I saw God face to face, and yet my life was spared.'

The sun rose above him as he passed Peniel, and he was limping because of his hip."

## Faith and Identity

It's important to note that, first and foremost, Jacob's encounter with God is an opportunity for faith to be born. This is at the very heart of the encounter. And this is identified, in part, by the question-and-response taking place. God (in the form of a man) asks Jacob for his name during the course of their wrestling match. And Jacob responds, "Jacob." This question-and-response relates back to the very deception performed by Jacob when accepting the blessing from his father. Remember, Jacob was asked twice by his father regarding his name, and Jacob replied that his name was Esau. Jacob was essentially denying his own identity in that moment.

So in his wrestling match with God, Jacob is asked again, "What is your name?" This question carries heavy implications, because answering correctly is not just a simple matter of identification. It involves an overall identity and acknowledgement of the sin that has been enacted under the name of Jacob. What's more is that, in ancient Jewish culture, a person's name carried more meaning and significance than a name given in modern times. It signified not just identity but character as well.

So why is God asking Jacob for his name? Well, again, the question in one sense is a challenge. Jacob's wrestling with God is a confrontation with God. It's a 'gospel' of sorts that demands a response. It's an *opportunity for Jacob to produce a response of faith.* And in order for this to happen, Jacob has to acknowledge his identity and all the baggage and sin that comes along with it. Jacob does this by responding differently than he did with his father. And when Jacob responds this time that his name is "Jacob," God then blesses him and changes his name to "Israel," signifying a 'new creation,' a new 'identity.' Just as we are new creations in Christ when we embrace the gospel (2 Corinthians 5:17), so was Jacob a new creation in God.

This name change, this identity change, is also important beyond the personal faith of Jacob. Israel wasn't just *Jacob's* new name; it was the name later given to God's people as a whole (i.e., Israel, or the Israelites). Therefore,

God's people are those who wrestle with Him and put their faith in Him: "Your name will no longer be Jacob, but Israel, because you have struggled with God and with humans and have overcome" (Genesis 32:28). As Christians, and with the scope of God's people expanding across all nationalities and cultures, we aren't 'Israelites' in the literal sense of the word. But figuratively speaking, we are. We are those who genuinely wrestle with God and all that He means. We are those who, in the midst of our wrestling, embrace a new identity in Christ, one that reflects God's image, one that is combating the sin in our lives which attempts to pull us from the vocation that God has for us. As theologian and scholar, N.T. Wright, states: "...sin is the rebellion of humankind against the vocation to reflect God's image into the world, the refusal to worship God the Creator, and the replacement of that worship and that vocation with the worship of elements of the created order...".[11]

## *Wrestling*

The physical wrestling that takes place within this story is also important. Jacob was wrestling *internally*. So the *act* of wrestling with God served as a mirror of what was taking place within him. You see, prior to his encounter with God, Jacob had created a life of chaos. And

---

[11] N.T. Wright, *Evil and the Justice of God*, (Downers Grove, IL: InterVarsity Press, 2006).

he knew that the blessings of God represent *divine order* in life, where relationships are reconciled and life itself is under the care and direction of God. Jacob wanted these blessings, and he wanted them on his terms. So before Jacob is asked his name, Jacob demands God's blessings. And Jacob's demand is telling of the human experience; because we all do this. We all desire God's blessings. But we want to obtain them in a way that allows us to maintain authority and control of our lives. So...*we wrestle with Him*. And God graciously allows this wrestling to happen with the hope of producing faith. Or as mentioned previously, if faith is already alive within the individual, the hope or process is to deepen this faith (deepen this relationship).

It's amazing how powerful the symbolic nature of Jacob's wrestling actually is. Despite the damage Jacob had caused with his life, he nevertheless maintained a desire for control. It didn't matter what he had done, or the mess he had made, the desire for control was still alive and well. But in order to genuinely embrace God, the desire for control must be released. This was true for Jacob, and it's true for us. Control is perhaps the single most prominent factor in our wrestling with God. We want to save ourselves and determine our own destiny. However, Jesus proclaims, "Whoever wants to save their life will lose it, but whoever loses their life for me will find it" (Matthew 16:25; Mark 8:35; Luke 9:24).

Part of the difficulty in releasing control pertains to its unnatural ability. Within our human nature is the desire and pursuit of control. In fact, according to contemporary research, *control* is included in the three categories of interpersonal needs alongside *inclusion* and *affection*.[12] Inclusion is the need to be included, to socialize with and be interesting to others. Affection is the need to feel loved and cared for. And control is right up there in the triad of interpersonal needs. It's the need to feel responsible for oneself, the ability to govern oneself and to influence others. To give up control in response to God's confrontation with our lives is altogether unnatural; yet it is altogether necessary.

A very inspiring way in which to look at this, and combined with the previous section which talks about assuming the identity of the Israelite (the wrestler) is through the story of Jesus as told in the Gospel of John. John inputs a beautiful theme of Jesus as the culmination of creation. Notice that John's opening lines ("In the beginning was the Word...") offer a re-telling of the creation story through Jesus. In the ancient world (particularly Jewish life) Sunday was the beginning of the week – a new week for new things, new possibilities, new life. Therefore, when Jesus rises on Sunday, according to John, He is a model of the 'new creation,' the new human being, the new direction God is taking humanity and,

---

[12] Melanie Booth-Butterfield, *Interpersonal Essentials* ($1^{st}$ ed.), (2001, Boston, MA: Pearson Publishing).

eventually, all of creation. Jesus is the embodiment of redemption. He *is* new creation. And when we surrender our lives to Him, He offers Himself and begins to create in us a new creation reflective of Him and His goodness.

## Wrestling with an Injury

Notice, also, that Jacob's hip is impaired in the very beginning of their wrestling match. Therefore, Jacob wasn't merely wrestling with God; he was wrestling with an injury. How this relates to us is that we're all injured in our personal encounters with God. In short, our wrestling with God takes place within a life that has been affected by sin. Furthermore, all of us have experienced some level of pain and suffering in this life. So sin is not just personal; it's cosmic. It infects all of life. Pain, in particular, is the dichotomy in our effort with God. It both pulls us *away* from Him at times as well as draws us *to* Him. But when we choose to embrace God, the pain we have experienced turn into scars. God heals our pain but the pain leaves its mark, and we do not forget it. The scars serve as a reminder of our commitment to Him.

The concept of scars alone is powerful. The average person most likely views scars as something negative, or perhaps signs of imperfection. But, as Christians, the significance of scars should remind us of the risen Jesus Christ. When we read the end of the gospel narratives we discover Jesus, raised from the dead. He has a new, perfect body – a template of the body we will all receive as Christians when we are raised with Him in the next life. And yet this new, perfect body still has its scars. Jesus still has the scars in His hands and feet from being nailed to the cross. And remember that it's not until the disciple Thomas sees and touches the scars of Jesus that he believes in Him (John 20:24-28). Scars are not marks of imperfection; they're indicators and reminders of where we have come from. They identify a past that is relevant to the future in which we are headed.

## *The Initiation of God and Love*

One of the most remarkable theological aspects of this story relates to the fact that God (not Jacob) is the initiator of the wrestling match. A core theme within Christian theology is that God is the initiator of salvation, or in simpler terms, relationship. In other words, it is not us who walk through life and at some point decide to turn toward God in pursuit of reconciliation. Such a turn simply isn't possible without the grace of God. Once God confronts us with His grace, only then are we capable of responding to Him. In short, *God is the initiator of the wrestling match for each of our lives.*

And why does God initiate? He initiates out of love; because God *is* love (1 John 4:8). This is altogether unique when we consider other religious and philosophical conceptions of God. The God of the Bible is not the god of the philosophers, for instance. With the god of the philosophers we find an immovable being, unwilling (if not unable) to interact with the world and its people. He's the 'unmoved mover' of Aristotle, a god who simply is, and exists merely to ponder his own existence. But with the God of the Bible we find a being of love, a personal being, a God who is dynamic and creative and seeks not only to engage the world and its people as the Creator, but furthermore seeks relationship with His created people. The god of the philosophers is indifferent to us, whereas the God of the Bible pursues us in love. The God of the Bible finds us so valuable that He is willing to wrestle with us and our confusion, pain, and uncertainties. The God who wrestled with Jacob is the same God who wrestles with us. What's more is that, if the Christian gospel is true (and I wholeheartedly believe that it is), then the God of the Bible is not just willing to wrestle with us, He is willing to die for us. And He did so two thousand years ago.

## *Conclusion*

There is much more practical theology and understanding that can be uncovered in the story of Jacob wrestling with God. But hopefully enough has been discussed in order to garner at least an adequate understanding of how this story sets the biblical and foundational tone for the faith of a wrestler. However, one of the amazing things about the Bible is that it doesn't just leave us with the story of Jacob. If the faith of a wrestler truly is the best approach to living and communicating the truth of Christianity, is there an example of how to live out the faith of a wrestler?

It's in the New Testament that we find the perfect example of the faith of a wrestler, and we find it in the person of Jesus Christ. In short, when it comes to wrestling with the fallen aspect of life, *Jesus was the greatest wrestler of all time.*

# THEY'RE JUST NOT INTERESTED

# CHAPTER 4

# JESUS THE WRESTLER

When we think of Jesus, His "wrestling" abilities are not typically considered. But the truth is that He was the greatest wrestler who ever lived. In fact, recognizing Jesus in this way is important as we look to Him for guidance in this life – a life which can prove to be difficult and uncertain.

## *An Uncomfortable Question*

When I started my studies in theology, the very first class I took was called "Life and the Teachings of Jesus" taught by Dr. Paul Eddy. This class transformed my thinking about Jesus as well as my understanding of what it means to be in relationship with Him. Toward the beginning of the semester, Dr. Eddy posed a question to the class. He asked, "What might be your immediate feelings and reaction if I suggested that Jesus made mistakes when he first started his career as a carpenter?"

Admittedly, the question caused me to feel really uncomfortable. And I'm sure my fellow classmates felt uncomfortable, too. You see, even though it's not a question of *moral* perfection, we tend to express perfection upon Jesus in all things, to the point that we only see Him as this divine figure. But when we do this, we disregard His humanness, and lose sight of how much He truly became a part of our human experience.

*Wrestling* is a significant part of the human experience. Struggle, temptation, suffering, and the wrestling we must do with them, are all a part of this. Again, Jesus, within the context of wrestling with the fallen aspects of life, was the greatest wrestler of all time. We often highlight the divinity of Jesus; but we can't dismiss His humanity. Jesus was both *fully* God (fully divine) and *fully* human. And it's within the context of His humanity that He embraces our experience. His confrontation with temptation, specifically, is what seems to draw this authentic experience out. Think about it. If Jesus was never tempted, how human was He? If Jesus never experienced what it feels like to be approached by temptation, if He never *wrestled* with temptation, if He never had to make a choice in order to overcome it, how human was He? Hebrews 4:15 states that God knows our weakness because in Christ He was tempted in all the same ways we are. This is vital in grasping our connectedness to Jesus.

## *The Temptation Story*

There's no better way to garner understanding of the above than to allow scripture to speak for itself. If temptation and our wrestling with it is truly an authentic aspect of the human experience, then it is no surprise that the "temptation story" in the gospels takes place prior to Jesus' mission to the cross. In order to be our advocate, in order to take our place, Jesus had to fully embrace our experience; and temptation is a significant part of this.

Luke 4:1-13 reads as follows: "Jesus, full of the Holy Spirit, left the Jordan and was led by the Spirit into the wilderness, where for forty days he was tempted by the devil. He ate nothing during those days, and at the end of them he was hungry.

The devil said to him, 'If you are the Son of God, tell this stone to become bread.'

Jesus answered, 'It is written: Man shall not live on bread alone.'

The devil led him up to a high place and showed him in an instant all the kingdoms of the world. And he said to him, 'I will give you all their authority and splendor; it has been given to me, and I can give it to anyone I want to. If you worship me, it will all be yours.'

Jesus answered, 'It is written: Worship the Lord your God and serve him only.'

The devil led him to Jerusalem and had him stand on the highest point of the temple. 'If you are the Son of God,' he said, 'throw yourself down from here. For it is written:

He will command his angels concerning you to guard you carefully;
they will lift you up in their hands, so that you will not strike your foot against a stone.'

Jesus answered, 'It is said: 'Do not put the Lord your God to the test.'

When the devil had finished all this tempting, he left him until an opportune time."

There are three specific temptations administered by the devil and they represent those that we all face and wrestle with to some degree. The *first temptation* Jesus faces is that of the physical – the physical suffering and weakness produced by hunger. However, it also embodies the temptation we encounter to fulfill our physical desires. All human beings have physical desires of which they are tempted to satisfy. Most men, for instance, have a sexual desire of sorts. Some struggle with this desire and temptation prior to marriage and have unfortunately engaged in sexual acts apart from a personal commitment of love, let alone marriage. And even those who are married still struggle with this temptation and have chosen to respond to it in a sinful manner by fulfilling their desire outside the marriage covenant. Another example pertaining to physical desire might be money. It's not that money itself is evil; but it is nevertheless a physical temptation which can lead to sin. As the scriptures tell us: "The love of money is a root of all kinds of evil" (1 Timothy 6:10). The emphasis of course is on the word "love," which is an inappropriate and godless response to money.

    Truth be told, this temptation is rampant within the American, Christian community. Look no further than today's televangelists and their large following who advocate a life of health, wealth and prosperity as evidence of God's blessings in a Christian's life. Not only is such a thing absurd, but those who engage in this type of faith end up never letting go of their focus and love for their physical desires.

    All in all, this first temptation addresses people's temptation to feed their selfishness in the form of their earthly desires. And how does Jesus respond? He says, "It is written: 'man shall not live on bread alone.'" In other words, we are more than flesh and bone. We are also spiritual beings made in the image of our Creator, and our spiritual health is even more vital. It's not that the body is unimportant in God's creation. After all, He did create us with a physical body and these bodies have innate desires. The body is good; but the spirit of God in union with our human spirit is what should be driving us (Romans 8:4-16). We should be seeking after *Him* above all else.

The *second temptation* refers to the human desire for authority and recognition. There is a desire within the human will to seek after praise. This includes people's temptation to seek after self-righteousness. It relates to the desire to *be as God*. And a number of theologians throughout the centuries have suggested that this temptation is the same temptation that Adam and Eve were approached with in the Garden of Eden. That is, the very first temptation human beings were confronted with, the temptation that eventually brought sin and death into the world, was this very temptation that Jesus faced in the wilderness. As a result, Jesus is essentially redoing the Garden experience. And where Adam and Eve failed and turned temptation into sin, Jesus succeeds.

So how does Jesus respond to this temptation? He says, "It is written: 'Worship the Lord your God and serve him only.'" In other words, there is only one God to whom all authority, praise and recognition belong.

The *third temptation* is related to the second. It refers to the human desire for power and glory, and the attempt

to manipulate God in order to achieve this. Every person tries to develop their own plans and goals for their life. They create their own blueprint and attempt to use God in order to achieve the goals outlined within it.
Corresponding to this, a pastor whom I deeply respect mentioned in a sermon that my generation, specifically, appears to be more narcissistic and focused on ourselves. We have no problem with talking about our personal goals and dreams in life – "This is what I'm going to do, and this is how I'm going to do it." But where's God in this? Was He ever consulted regarding your plans?

When we do this, when we disregard God's power and direction in our lives, we end up with a self-infused blueprint worth essentially nothing. When we do this, the objective is not to seek God for guidance; the objective is to make God fit into our life's blueprint however *we* see fit. This addresses people's temptation to fulfill their selfishness in the form of control. And we saw this very issue in the previous chapter which discussed Jacob wrestling with God. Jacob wanted God's blessings, but he wanted to obtain them in a way that allowed him to maintain authority and control of his life. The same is true for every human being who has ever lived.

So how does Jesus respond to this temptation? He states, "It is said: 'Do not put the Lord your God to the test.'" In other words, forget your blueprint! God is not a resource to be manipulated.

## *Good Friday*

Of course, when we talk about "Jesus the Wrestler," we cannot forget the temptation He experienced in choosing to face death on the cross. In the Garden of Gethsemane Jesus wrestled with the temptation of resisting His destiny to endure the cross and all the pain and suffering leading up to it. In fact, the scriptures tell us that He experienced so much emotional anguish that He bled beads of sweat (Luke 22:44). Yet in the midst of temptation, Jesus chose to heed to the Father's will and embrace all that awaited Him.

We refer to Jesus' death on the cross as "Good Friday." And while the picture of His torture and death doesn't appear to be "good," we also know that His death on the cross must be seen in light of His subsequent resurrection. In other words, it's because of the resurrection that the cross is filled with meaning. The death of Jesus becomes a victory. That is, the power of the resurrection vanquishes and claims victory over all that Jesus carried with Him to the cross and all that died with Him on it. The sin and evil of the world was carried on the shoulders of Jesus and was conquered in His death (1 Peter 2:24). *This* is the goodness of Good Friday. The goodness of God claimed victory over sin and evil through the death of Jesus Christ. And because of this we have the opportunity to overcome the divide that once separated us from relationship with God.

## *Embracing the Faith of a Wrestler*

Hopefully a better understanding of what the faith of a wrestler looks like has been acquired – both in the story of Jacob (found in the previous chapter) as well as the story of Jesus. Jacob's struggle is our struggle. All the theological underpinnings of this story reflect the human predicament in relation to God. And we find a perfect display of the faith of a wrestler in the life of Jesus, specifically as revealed in the temptation story as well as the temptation He experienced prior to His death on the cross. Jesus revealed an unwavering dependence on God the Father despite the various temptations he encountered to do otherwise. Perhaps even my own story, shared in the beginning of the previous chapter resonates, in that it captured somewhat the nature and difficulty of life and faith – the ups and downs, the triumphs and defeats.

In simplistic terms, the faith of a wrestler acknowledges that life is not easy, and that it is perfectly acceptable to admit that we don't have all the answers. It acknowledges that central to faith in God is *relationship*. And in a relationship is genuine struggle at times. This is true for any relationship whether it be a spouse, a brother, a sister, or a friend. Relationship, on this side of heaven, will entail moments of joy as well as moments of struggle. Sometimes our wrestling with God includes periods of doubt or confusion regarding personal hardship, and sometimes it's merely brought on by a desire to know God more and be a more passionate disciple of Jesus Christ. This chapter and the previous set the foundation for the faith of a wrestler. But let's dig deeper.

# THEY'RE JUST NOT INTERESTED

# CHAPTER 5

# WRESTLING AND RELATIONSHIP

The conclusion of chapter 4 suggested that *wrestling* implies *relationship*. And that's the focus of this current chapter. One of the most unique elements of the Christian faith is that it advocates for a *relationship* with the God of the universe as opposed to a life of strict adherence to religious law or doctrine. This is profoundly different than the framework of other faiths. And if the Christian faith is going to advocate for a relationship with God, it needs to be understood that *wrestling* is central to relationship – for better or worse. Within any given relationship is going to be wrestling. What's more is that we do the most wrestling with the relationships we deem most important. In fact, by nature, human beings are prone to avoid conflict or engage in genuine struggle unless the person is deemed worth engaging in conflict with. And wrestling in a relationship is not just about the decided importance of the relationship, it also includes the potential that the wrestling will lead to deeper intimacy and a growing level of trust.

*Trust* is an essential part of developing a relationship. And since the Christian faith is advocating for a relationship with God, it should come as no surprise that trust is a repeated element in the scriptures (Jeremiah 17:7-8; Proverbs 3:5-6; 16:3; Psalm 56:3; 143:8; etc.). According to communication and sociology scholar, Melanie Booth-Butterfield, "Interpersonal trust is an individual's characteristic belief that the sincerity, benevolence, or truthfulness of others can generally be relied on."[13] What does this mean? First of all, it means that *trust* is a *belief system*. We put our trust in those whom we *believe* to be trustworthy. Secondly, it means that trust is something that can either grow or wane. Based on our interaction in any given relationship, our trust can grow due to trust being upheld by the person with whom it was given; or it can wane due to the person violating or not upholding the trust that was given.

## *Relationship with Jesus Christ*

It's a peculiar thing, even for many Christians: that is, Christianity claims that we can have a relationship with God through the person of Jesus Christ. Think about it. We are claiming to have a relationship with a person who was

---

[13] Melanie Booth-Butterfield, *Interpersonal Essentials* (1st ed.).

God in the flesh, a person who died two thousand years ago, but a person who resurrected from the dead and is no longer dead but alive...though we can't see Him. Yet as strange as it might sound, this is the very reason for our proclamation of relationship with God. In order to have a relationship with someone, he or she must be living. And we claim that Jesus is in fact living (He is risen!). So even though we can't *see* Him, we nevertheless *experience* Him through the power of the Holy Spirit. In other words, the Spirit of God is the witness of Jesus' life. If we're honest, there's no *rational* explanation for this.

Now, let me clarify that I don't believe the Christian faith to be a faith of irrational charismatics. I do believe, when people engage the claims of Christianity, they will find lots of reasonable answers. For instance, there is substantial evidence in support of the reliability of the Bible as well as its depiction of Jesus and His claims. I even believe that there is reasonable evidence to suggest that Jesus actually resurrected from the dead. But the reality is that people are motivated not simply by means of what information can be gained intellectually. People are not simply motivated toward belief by working through historical, scientific, or philosophical evidence. As I have consistently proposed throughout this book, belief is not so much a matter of intellectual assent. There are multiple aspects at play when it comes to belief, and it takes the whole person to step into the realm of belief, not just their mind. Moreover, this step is a commitment.

With that said, and while I don't think the Christian faith to be a faith of irrational charismatics, I also don't believe that it is a faith of intellectuals. Instead, it's a faith for all those who are lost and seeking. It's a faith that connects to the very heart of every human being who has ever lived. It connects to the real things of life. Unfortunately, Christian theologians have been so enamored with sustaining Christian doctrine that they have sadly lost sight of the purpose of the gospel in the first place, which is to offer the 'good news' of Jesus Christ who has come to save the lost. Doctrine is important. It can help guide us in sustaining the health and character of the church as well as our understanding of God. However, if a focus on doctrine is keeping us from reaching the lost, then it's high time we loosen the reins. Not so that people can insert whatever they feel like, but so that doctrine becomes a guiding tool rather than a rule of law in declaring who is a Christian and who is not. After all, how many Christians are proficient in Christian doctrine? The answer: very few! Does that mean the vast majority of Christians are not really Christians at all, or that God's saving work on the cross will only accomplish saving those who have acquired proficiency in Christian doctrine? I hardly think so! Faith in Christ is the cornerstone of God's salvation, not our ability to understand, communicate and uphold doctrine.

## Confronted with Faith on a Plane

I'm reminded of a story I heard from my local pastor – Pastor Rod. Years ago, he was heading to a Christian conference, and on the plane, the lady sitting next to him was returning from a Benny Hinn event. For those unfamiliar with Mr. Hinn, he is a wildly charismatic televangelist who contains a large following. He refers to himself as a modern prophet, and claims to have the power to perform miracles, particularly the power of healing. The lady was very boisterous and introduced herself to Rod and asked him what he does for a living. Rod told her that he is a pastor. "Praise the Lord!" She yelled. She continued to talk with Rod as the plane took off, telling him about Benny Hinn and the wonderful things that God was doing at the event. Rod was familiar with Mr. Hinn and found him to be somewhat obnoxious as well as his ministry a bit damaging to the Christian cause. After a while, the lady could see that Rod was losing interest in the conversation, and so she turned to the man sitting on the other side of her: a business man adorned in a suit and tie. As the lady talked to the business man about God, Jesus, and so on, Rod focused on his work. However, he still felt a little uncomfortable as he assumed the business man – most likely an intelligent gentleman – was probably wishing the lady would leave him alone.

Several minutes past, and the lady was still talking with the business man. All the sudden, the lady tapped

Rod on the shoulder. "Rod, I'd like you to meet John. John just accepted Jesus into his heart!"

Rod looked up and saw the man staring at him with tears running down his face. Immediately, Rod felt a sense of surprise and confusion. He thought for sure that a charismatic, Christian kook like this lady would drive the business man insane. But as it turns out, her approach may have been just what that man needed in order to embrace his own faith and relationship with Jesus Christ.

## *Do You Know Jesus?*

Whether a lay Christian, pastor or scholar, we can all get caught up in the things that surround the Christian faith and lose sight of our focus on the one thing (the one person) that matters: Jesus. The Bible, for instance, is an incredible resource for us as a Christian community in striving to understand and follow God. We should be eternally grateful for it! But the Bible itself is *not* God. The Bible is *not* Jesus. Let me put it this way: You may know the Bible, but do you know Jesus? You may know Christian doctrine, but do you know Jesus?

These questions, at first, might seem confusing. And if so, perhaps that's the problem! A number of Christians have found it difficult to make a distinction between the written word (the Bible) and the Word Himself (Jesus). So much so that they have become enamored with scripture, and interpretations of scripture, and forgotten to engage the very God to whom the scriptures speak of! Scripture is a *witness* to the God we worship, not God Himself. We are in a relationship with *Christ*, not the Bible, not biblical interpretation, not doctrine.

All of this should lend our thoughts to the third person of the Trinity: the Holy Spirit. In reality, the Spirit should be our greatest resource in knowing and experiencing God. The Spirit brings the scriptures to life. And apart from the Bible, the Spirit is a living, moving, and engaging part of the Godhead. The Spirit can speak through the Bible, and does. But the Spirit does not need the Bible in order to stir the hearts of people, nor does the Spirit need the Bible in order to transform their lives. The primary role of the Spirit is to awaken hearts to the truth of Jesus and His salvation. The Spirit shines a glorious light upon the *relationship* with God that awaits all those who respond to His prompting, and is able to aid us through life as we strive to follow Jesus.

If what the Christian faith is offering is merely some philosophy of life, then by all means, let's continue living our faith as is and communicate to others about the gospel by means of appealing to their minds. If the Christian faith is simply offering religious zealots the opportunity to learn and grow in their knowledge of doctrine, then by all means, let's continue living our faith as is, barricade ourselves inside our little theological communities and make judgments about who is in and who is out, and communicate to others that Christianity is for a small group of theologically astute people. If it's merely offering a self-help guide for people to "live their best life now,"[14] then by all means, let's continue living our faith as is and communicate to others that God's blessings come in the form of material health and wealth as well as a life free of troubles. But the truth is that the Christian faith is not really any of these things.

The gospel is not offering a mere philosophy of life. It's not only for the doctrinally inclined. It's not a self-help guide to "live your best life now." It's not even some spiritual resource and guide to become a "good" or "better" person. The gospel is "good news;" it's the proclamation of King Jesus – that God has arrived in the person of Jesus, that He has overcome, that He has conquered, that He has reclaimed His creation, that He will one day redeem all of it, that He has brought salvation to the world, and most importantly to us, that we are invited to be a part of His redemptive purposes. God's work in redeeming individual lives is a glimpse into the redemption of all of creation. The goodness that comes out of a redeemed person's life is a foreshadowing of the goodness that will reign in all the world when Jesus returns again and completes what He has started.

---

[14] Joel Osteen, *Your Best Life Now: 7 Steps to Living at Your Full Potential* (New York, NY: FaithWords, 2004).

The Christian faith is about God, that He desires relational union with His human creations and that He has made this available through the person of Jesus. In other words, because of Jesus we are invited to be in relationship with God and align with His good purposes. The Christian faith is *relationship*.

Do you know Jesus?

## To Be Known

I contemplated organizing this next section into a chapter all its own. But the concept is so deeply connected to the idea of divine relationship that it seemed fitting to keep it within this present chapter on relationship.

It's not uncommon for me to think about death. To be honest, I don't necessarily fear death in the sense that I'm scared of dying. It's the unknown that I fear – what lies on the other side, what it looks like, what to expect, and so forth. It's also strange to me to think about how we're here one moment – living, breathing, laughing, crying, worrying about the future – and the next moment we may not be. And once we're gone, there is of course a time of mourning on the part of those who loved us, but eventually life and its people move on.

Usually when my wife and I climb into bed at night, we give in to exhaustion rather quickly and fall asleep. We typically don't engage in deep philosophical or theological discussions, either. Or when we do, the discussions don't involve much mutual effort. Often times when I start sharing my thoughts on "the meaning of life," my wife eventually looks at me with a smile and says, "Okay, buddy. Let's settle down." But one particular night was different. For some reason, she decided to join me in my thoughts, and at a time when she probably would have much rather been sleeping.

She admitted her fear of death, and the type of fear she expressed was very interesting to me. "You know what scares me about death?" She said. "It's the idea that I won't be known anymore, that I'll be forgotten. People grieve the loss of a loved one, but eventually they move on, and I won't move on with them. For a while, I'll just be a memory. And over time, that memory fades."

Months ago I read an article relating to the very thought my wife shared with me. The article talked about how the current generation does not fear death in terms of judgment ("Was I a good person? Did I live a good life? Does heaven or hell await me?"). In other words, there is less of a moral component. The research supported in the article stated that today's generation fears death in a way much more related to my wife's sentiment. That is, they fear "not being known" once they exit this life. They fear "being forgotten." There were several reasons offered for this, and one of them pertains to a more favorable outlook on life after death. For instance, most people in our American culture contain a "universalist" view. That is, the average person believes in life after death, and also believes that virtually all people go to heaven; and if there is a hell, it's strictly for those "really bad" people: the Hitlers and Stalins of the world. And this is the case regardless of one's religious convictions. For example, there are also many Christians who contain a universalist mindset. And the mindset exists in varying degrees. For some, it's a deep seated belief, and for others it's merely an established hope. Again, there are of course other reasons for such a shift, but be that as it may, there is less a fear of moral judgment and more a fear of not being known, of being forgotten.

Should there be concern regarding the lack of consideration for morality (for judgment) when it comes to our embrace with death? Probably. But there is nevertheless something incredibly important about this fear of "not being known."

In Psalm 139:13, David writes to God, "…you created my inmost being; you knit me together in my mother's womb." And the prophet Jeremiah describes God saying to him, "'Before I formed you in the womb I knew you…'" (Jeremiah 1:5). As God's creation, each one of us is 'known' by Him. In fact, *before anyone else knew us, we were known by God*. And as God's creation, and since He covers *all* of life (including life after death), He still *knows* us once we have passed on from this world.

To be known is an unwavering desire within our hearts. But why? Why this desire (this need) to be known? And why such a fear in no longer being so?

It's my suggestion that all the countless desires within our hearts were divinely implanted by God as a means to draw us to Himself. As St. Augustine prayed, "You have made us for yourself, and our hearts are restless till they find their rest in you."[15] And this includes the desire to be known. I will discuss this again in a later chapter, but instead of following this desire to where it leads, we often fulfill it through our own means. That is, we set on a journey to fulfill this need, most prominently through our relationships with others. We develop a community around us – however big or small – and allow people to get to know us, like us, care for us, and love us. Yet the fulfillment is temporary; for we understand that life is temporary. In short, death is inevitable. And so instead of loosening fear's grip on us, we merely ignore it or tuck it away as far back as possible within the dark corners of our minds.

---

[15] *The Confessions of Augustine*, trans. S. E. Wirt (Grand Rapids, MI: Zondervan, 1971), 1.

However, instead of ignoring this fear, we should listen to it. While our relationships on this earth are wonderful (and hopefully many of them will continue on into eternity in heaven), this desire to be known, and our fear in not being so, should tell us more than we can imagine. After all, central to being known is *relationship*. And in God creating us, in God knowing us, *He desires for us to know Him in return.*

From a personal standpoint, I feel that I can say with confidence: I know God, and God knows me. And this is enough to stifle any fear that I might have in death. Though death will usher me into a mysterious realm, and one filled with plenty of unanswered questions, I know that Jesus will meet me there with enough love and assurance to calm my spirit.

Whether in life or death, the Christian faith is founded on relationship – relationship with the God of the universe through the person of Jesus Christ. The faith of a wrestler not only acknowledges the relational component to the faith, it fully embraces it and places it at the center of Christianity where it belongs.

THEY'RE JUST NOT INTERESTED

# CHAPTER 6

# FAMILY

I grew up in a blended family. And while I certainly loved and appreciated the experience of being a part of a large family, there is a sense in which I was the product of brokenness from the very beginning. That is, for each of my parents it was their second marriage; and so they found each other at a time when they were coming out of something broken.

My mother brought with her a daughter, and my father brought with him two daughters and a son. I was the first born of my parents – the first child who arrived into the blended family experiment. And then there were my two younger brothers. As would be expected, I knew very little of the issues that took place in our home in Liberty, Missouri. From a general perspective, I experienced all the joys a young boy should: I laughed, played, and got into mischief. All the difficulties that occurred during that time were, for the most part, outside the radar of my comprehension. But there was still a sense in which I understood that things were a little different for our family. A long court battle eventually resulted in losing two of my sisters for the remainder of my childhood years. They left when I was six years old to go live with their mom, and even though it was probably for the best, I missed out on the opportunity to know them better and develop a relationship with them.

My mother was a caregiver. I suppose most mothers are. Despite the odds against her, she had an unwavering desire to keep our family intact. Perhaps it was an attempt at making her amends for the failure in her first marriage, or perhaps she truly had a sincere passion for family. Whatever the case may be, I know that I inherited a significant part of my devotion to family from her. My father, on the other hand, was a complex figure. He was a unique version of Dr. Jekyll and Mr. Hyde – two personalities which, at times, caused you to question which personality was in fact the real one. He was incredibly loving, and yet incredibly violent. It was confusing, to say the least.

As most children do, I looked up to my father. I suppose at some point or another I wanted to be like him. Still, I couldn't make sense of the violence. Many times, there was no reason for it. His anger was like a sensitive twitch: if agitated even slightly, the whole thing would trigger. And there wasn't any sort of resolve, either, until he broke something or hurt someone. As long as he satisfied his rage in some manner, the rage would stop, and he would go back to showering us with love and affection. The irony is that I learned how to love, in part, as a result of my father's expressions of love for me. His hugs were the warmest, his strength the most comforting, and his words the most soothing for someone who needed to hear an affirming sense of affection.

I've mentioned already that the age of six was when I was introduced to the sport of wrestling. And of the hundreds of wrestling practices I have gone through in my life, I still remember my very first. I can still feel the humidity in the room, see the dim lights, and smell the musty room filled with the sweat of dozens of young wrestlers. For whatever reason, wrestling came naturally to me. My family apparently couldn't afford actual wrestling shoes at the time, so I won my first tournament wearing white tennis-shoes: shoes better suited for a basketball court than a wrestling mat. It didn't matter all that much, though. So much of wrestling at that age is a mixture of running into each other, grabbing a hold of something (or engaging in a bear hug) and seeing who is the first to fall on their back. Occasionally you would see a perfectly executed takedown, but it wasn't necessarily the norm.

My older brother, Brad, and younger brother, Richard, also started wrestling around that time. And with the youngest (Joseph) eventually making his way to the mat, I suppose you could say that we were a legitimate "wrestling family." The sport was a part of the very makeup of our family unit. So much so, that we spent many a weekend traveling the Midwest (and farther at times) in order to compete in the best tournaments available. The pinnacle of all wrestling tournaments for kids was Tulsa Nationals held in Tulsa, Oklahoma. The tournament was toward the middle of the season, and, by far, the toughest in the country. Only the best young wrestlers even so much as placed in the tournament. I won several AAU and Cliff Keen national titles as a kid, but the best I ever did in Tulsa was a fifth place finish.

Brad was much older, so we rarely had the privilege of him traveling with us. He also didn't start wrestling until junior high, so his progression in the sport required a quicker pace. And he was successful in that progression, eventually earning a second place finish in the Missouri state championships as a senior before moving on to compete in college at the Naval Academy. I looked up to him. I admired his drive and passion. But unfortunately, due to the age gap, much of the family structure involved just mom, dad, Richard, Joseph, and I.

These times of wrestling travel and competition contain some of the fondest memories of my family, and my father in particular. Though complex as he was, it was at wrestling tournaments when I felt close to him. Before every match, he would pick me up in his arms, squeeze tight, and whisper in my ear, "Give it all you got. Win or lose, I still love you." In those moments, I never questioned his sincerity. And I also tended to experience a great deal of nervousness prior to matches, so this ritual with my father was important to me. It may have not settled my nerves completely, but it did provide a hint of calm when it was needed. My mother and father split when I was in high school, and sometime after that, my relationship with my father ended. But while I no longer have an ongoing relationship with him, I still look back at this time in our lives positively.

Even as particularly intricate and broken as my family was (and is), I love my family. Within my heart is an attachment to each person, despite being in a place in life in which I am growing my own family with my wife and two children. In fact, it is my belief that our natural affection and desire for familial togetherness is a product of God's design in us. After all, it is the Christian belief that God is in the work of redeeming His human creatures and bringing them together so as to adopt them into His own family (the church). God is our father (and mother). We are His children. And to one another, we are brothers and sisters in Him. We long for community, for family, because the desire has been suffused in us by our Creator. There are certainly those who live as exceptions to this natural leaning toward family, who repulse their family and who desire to be independent from any such unity; but they are in fact *exceptions*. Most people, to some varying degree, contain an internal thrust and commitment toward this sort of community.

Of course, on this side of heaven, God's family is just as dysfunctional as our biological ones. Though we long for unity, we usually fail in bringing it about; hence, the hundreds of denominations that have transpired on account of ecclesial bickering and tantrums, as well as the many people who have rejected the church as a result of being treated poorly. But does this mean that God or His family is a colossal counterfeit? Of course not! When dysfunction happens within biological families, do we conclude that the family system is fake or a product of some fairy tale ideal? The reality is that we simply accept the fact that brokenness is a part of the family system, and that each family is trying to overcome the brokenness that is apparent in their own. Just because something is broken doesn't mean we abandon it. Some things are worth saving. Some things are worth our blood, sweat and tears. Family, and the unity that we desire within it, is worth it.

## *God is Love*

Christian author and apologist, C. S. Lewis, had a magnificent ability to communicate complex theological ideas in a way that simplified them so that the average person could understand. I think his explanation of the concept of 'God is love' to be an example of this.

> All sorts of people are fond of repeating the Christian statement that "God is love". But they seem not to notice that the words "God is love" have no real meaning unless God contains at least two Persons. Love is something that one person has for another person. If God was a single person, then before the world was made, He was not love. Of course, what these people mean when they say that God is love is often something quite different: they really mean "Love is God". They really mean that our feelings of love, however and wherever they arise, and whatever results they produce, are to be treated with great respect. Perhaps they are: but that is something quite different from what Christians mean by the statement "God is love". They believe that the living, dynamic activity of love has been going on in God forever and has created everything else.[16]

What's important to identify here is that, by understanding God is love, we are recognizing Him as a living, dynamic community within Himself. And that the love within this Trinitarian God/community is the very source which created. It is the very source which brought humanity into existence. And in recognizing this, we come to find that creation was enacted with purpose – that is, to invite His created personal beings (humans) into

---

[16] C.S. Lewis, *Mere Christianity: Signature Classics Edition*, (New York, NY: HarperOne, 1980).

community with Him. In other words, the living, dynamic community of love that has been alive for eternity past has reached outside of Himself in order to invite others to partake in His eternal love. Or to put this even more simply, God created in order to adopt a family!

## *Desire*

Continuing with this present theme, I want to expound upon this idea of desire(s). Our desires for true love and for family are not products of wishful thinking but are aspects within our being that tell a much bigger story.

There appear to be two sides to human conduct: (1) the desirable, and (2) the actual. It's rather clear to me that we as individual human beings wish we lived life a certain way. And yet, the wish – the imagined life that should be – isn't. I was reminded of this when listening to a song on the radio. Recently I have been in the habit of listening to lyrics more closely; and this particular song struck me by the forgiveness and subsequent promises that the lyrics advocated. It was a "love song;" but not the kind merely professing an individual's unrivaled love for another – the angel from heaven who fell into the lap of a longing soul, the flawless beauty who just so happened to cross paths with someone searching for true love. Nor was it one of those songs in which the person is expressing their love for another after he or she has lost them, after the relationship has ended and the person is in anguish, desperate to win their lover back. The song I heard was somewhere in between these two facets of romantic melody. It was a man's proclamation to forgive the failures and sins of the woman he loves. The man suggests that he is unaffected by any of her mistakes, that he doesn't care about them, that all that matters is that he loves her. He accepts her for who she is; promises to never hold her problematic history against her. Instead of judgment, the man promises a clean slate, an opportunity to start all over. And he proclaims, with assurance, that he will love her perfectly.

Now the sad thing is that the above consists of mere words – a simple vision and hope of which we aspire. Very few (if any) truly live in such a way that freely expresses love and forgiveness so perfectly. We may do so *im*perfectly, in the sense that we remain faithful and true to our spouses or significant others. But it probably doesn't look like the perfect picture our songs portray. The truth is that we all have moments of selfishness. We experience times in which forgiveness is too hard to offer; and even when we do offer it, we are still affected by the pain and sadness that the other person's actions caused us. We experience a lapse in judgment as well as weakness and vulnerability. We get defensive. At times, we even lose sight of who we are. In short, if left to our own devices, we are incredible failures.

But this doesn't dismiss the fact that we still desire something better. If we didn't yearn for perfect love and unity, we wouldn't write songs about it. We would simply accept reality for what it is; and reality, unfortunately, is somewhat disappointing. After all, who is living the life that we sing about? Who is, with no apparent trouble, actually loving another person without succumbing to selfish moments? Who is so emotionally proficient that they are unscathed by the hurt their significant other may cause them? It's certainly not me! Nevertheless, the inherent desires within us of perfect love exist, and we consistently profess them. Even more so, we yearn for them.

There are many reasons why I believe the Bible to be God-breathed. Some are more convincing than others. A reason which lies more in a personal discovery involves the Bible's ability to illustrate a picture of our deepest longings as a human race. When people are able to look past the unfamiliar cultural milieu and past the obscure theology, they come to find something real and true about what their soul is longing for. There is something about our desires for love, heaven and family that find their purpose in the biblical story. Not only do we discover where the desires began, but we obtain some inkling of an understanding of why we have them and where they are meant to lead us.

## THEY'RE JUST NOT INTERESTED

This present world, and our fallen human condition within it, is not all there is. The desires of our soul are desires attached to something real. In other words, it's not the case that our desires are products of wishful thinking, or a crutch to aid us through life in order to combat the evil and confusion we experience in this world. Our desires are built within us; they're a part of us. They serve as subtle reminders pointing us toward home. And when we follow the direction of these soulful desires, we find that there's a whole new world out there; we just haven't fully arrived there yet. But when we do, these desires will experience fulfillment. They will no longer be, because the pulling that these desires have been performing on our hearts has finally accomplished its intention. We will be in heaven – a perfect union of love and community, of family.

In some way, I think this is what the biblical story (the Christian faith) is all about. We're born into a strange world, a world some of us feel alien to. And while we experience moments of comfort and happiness, we have this sense that there's more to the story than what we've noticed thus far, that perhaps this world is merely a segue into another, and one far more satisfying and magnificent than the present. Within this realization, we recognize that there must be a God associated with this "other" world, that maybe it is He who created these very longings within our hearts in order to grab our attention. Perhaps He utilizes these desires in order to draw us toward Himself. In other words, perhaps God is constantly, by His spirit, pulling his toward Himself in order to lead us to where true love, community and heaven abide: Him.

There's a problem that we typically run into with regard to these desires, and it pertains to the belief of some that these desires can (and should) be made fully apparent in the present life. Simply put, the recognition of these desires becomes so strong that the person takes them and attempts to fulfill these desires through whatever means possible. For example, his or her sincere desire for true love becomes a mission of theirs to obtain complete fulfillment through another human being, particularly romantic in form. The problem, of course, is that the other person is a few steps short of perfection. They are unfortunately just as "human" and prone to make mistakes. As a result, he or she becomes increasingly disappointed and heart-broken over their failed mission to discover true love in this life. But the truth is that these desires were not necessarily meant for us to extract fulfillment from others. As alluded to already, these desires were meant to draw us to God – the only true source of perfect love. We should obviously strive to love one another perfectly. But this striving should be done with the understanding that genuine, perfect love and family are found in God alone. It should be done with the understanding that we are undoubtedly going to fail one another at times. It should be done with the understanding that we can always love one another *better*, but will never (in this life) love one another *perfectly*, in the truest sense of the word. And furthermore, we should understand that our striving to love one another perfectly is a process; it's preparation for our life in eternity. Simply put, it's a process of God's work in transforming us from naturally selfish individuals into humble individuals – individuals who give of themselves self-sacrificially.

These desires for true love and tranquility are expressed everywhere; not merely in songs but in films, books, speeches, and more. Though you can *ignore* them, you cannot *escape* them. The moment you begin to acknowledge them and ask the question of why these desires exist is the moment you start heading in the right direction. When you disregard them, or disparage them as the musings of ignorant people wishing for something better than reality, you are heading in a direction that actually proves to be unnatural. Whatever conclusions you make of these desires, it's rather difficult to dismiss them outright. There really is something to them.

## *A Heavenly Family*

The Christian faith is unlike any other religious faith in its relational component, and this has been heavily emphasized throughout this book. But despite the fact that we often talk about a relationship with God, we seem to so easily lose sight of the relational quality and foundation, and get distracted by other things. For instance, and as previously mentioned, we become infatuated with the written word (the Bible) as opposed to the Word Himself (Jesus). As a result, instead of utilizing the Bible as a resource to know Jesus more and grow in relationship with Him, we treat the Bible as a book of religious law, a rule book, and unintentionally, we treat it as essentially God Himself. And the many Christians who have fallen into this trap find themselves becoming judges of Christianity. That is, they develop a religious guideline with which to weed through the authentic and inauthentic Christians. Rather than truly embracing the relational quality of the Christian faith, they become overly concerned with deciphering who is in and who is out, who is actually a part of this divine family and who is not.

While proper theology or doctrine is important in order to sustain the character of God and His church, we are not the dictators or judges of His church. We are not the dictators and judges of other people's faith. Authentic faith according to the gospel of Christ is quite simple: To believe in the life, death and resurrection of Christ and to put our faith and trust in His salvific promise and power. If we decide to step in and suggest that 'proper thinking' (theology or doctrine) is necessary in order to enact God's salvation then we have severely overstepped our bounds.

Look, what we're dealing with here is a family – a heavenly family. And as imperfect human beings, we have an imperfect family. Imperfect families will undoubtedly breed dysfunction. Each member of the family is unique, and with unique thoughts and ideas about the Christian faith and their relationship with Christ. Some of these thoughts and ideas might be way off course. But does that mean the people themselves are not Christian? Does that mean they are not a part of the family?

## *The Thief on the Cross*

One of the most remarkable stories in the New Testament is "the thief on the cross." This story is found in the gospel of Luke when Jesus is nailed to the cross between two convicted criminals:

"One of the criminals who hung there hurled insults at him: 'Aren't you the Messiah? Save yourself and us!'

But the other criminal rebuked him. 'Don't you fear God,' he said, 'since you are under the same sentence? We are punished justly, for we are getting what our deeds deserve. But this man has done nothing wrong.'

Then he said, 'Jesus, remember me when you come into your kingdom.'

Jesus answered him, 'Truly I tell you, today you will be with me in paradise'" (Luke 23:39-43).

Did this thief nailed to a cross next to Jesus contain proper understanding of Christian doctrine? Did he think correctly regarding God and who He is? Of course not! He merely put His faith in Jesus. "Remember me," he says to Jesus. And apparently this was enough. This was a sufficient enough step of belief in the salvation of Jesus Christ.

# THEY'RE JUST NOT INTERESTED

# CHAPTER 7

# THIS IS LIFE

It is my belief that the faith of a wrestler is the most accurate description and approach to the Christian faith. Part of the reason for this is that the faith of a wrestler acknowledges reality. That is, it acknowledges that life isn't as it should be; the world isn't as it should. The influence of sin and evil is real and pervasive. Yes, it should be the belief of every Christian that God will eventually redeem His creation and everything in it. In other words, the end of the story reads: "God wins." However, we are in the midst of the story. We have not reached the end quite yet; and the middle of the story includes a tremendous amount of injustice, a tremendous amount of pain and suffering for many people. Of course we all experience pain and suffering in varying degrees. But be that as it may, reality is what it is. And a lot of times it's not pretty. It's a struggle. It's a never ending wrestling match.

This is not to take away from the goodness of God's creation. While the faith of a wrestler acknowledges that the reality of the world is a bit of a mess in serious need of repair, the goodness of God's creation is also very apparent and easy to find. It comes in many different forms. For instance, in nature, such as the beauty of the sunrise and sunset, the crashing waves upon sandy beaches, or the majestic mountains overlooking forests and creatures of all kinds. And we of course see God's goodness in our relationships here on earth, whether it be the romantic and committed love of a spouse, or the love of a brother, sister or a dear friend. The goodness of God's creation is everywhere and we can no more escape it than we can the impact of sin and evil.

But with that said, the faith of a wrestler does not belittle or disparage the idea that we live in a messed up world. It instead takes it seriously. Bad things happen to good people. Terrible things happen for no apparent reason. And we are left to wonder, at times, "God, where are you?"

In a culture in which it seems Christians are so quick to believe that God's plan for their life involves a high paying job, a hefty bank account and a life free of troubles, we need the faith of a wrestler more than ever. The vast majority of people are not experiencing the apparent "blessings" of God in the form of health, wealth and prosperity. Moreover, it seems to me that God could care less about how much money we make or what kind of job we have or how He can help establish us financially. For if it were in fact the case that God was in the job of such things, the early disciples and church must have missed the mark when they were hounded and murdered on account of their faith. Far from chasing after gold and a comfortable living, those in the early Christian church lived in constant fear for their lives. It seems to me that God is far more concerned with building up a group of people (His church) who are chasing after *Him* as He slowly but surely engages a process of transforming their lives. It seems to me that He is far more concerned with creating a family, one that resembles His goodness and love, one that looks like His son, Jesus.

## *When the World Falls Apart*

I have two children – a daughter and a son. However, what you may not know is that my daughter is from a previous marriage. I was in the midst of studying theology at Bethel University when I obtained my first job as a pastor. I was hired as the pastor of college ministry at a local church, along with serving part-time in areas of children's ministry as well as worship for the youth ministry. At that time, I thought for sure that my career in the church was set.

However, only two months into my pastoral duties, my wife stated that we needed to talk. She had been a primary support for me in my pursuit of ministry, but for some reason grew very cold and distant once I was hired. As a result, I was already going through a great deal of confusion and pain prior to the conversation; but nevertheless I did not expect what came next.

"Mike," she said with a face bearing no expression, "I don't want to be a pastor's wife. I don't want to be married to you anymore. I've been thinking about this for several months and realized that I really don't love you...I never did."

I was in utter shock. I immediately got up and started pacing the room, trying my best to understand what was happening. But no matter what my mind could come up with, there was no way of rationalizing the horror of the predicament I was in.

That night, she took my daughter, walked out the door, and drove to her parents' house. She never came back.

It wasn't long afterwards that the church, in recognizing the personal turmoil I was going through, had me step down from my role. And truth be told, I didn't care. My life was in shambles. Far from being a leader in the church, I was dying inside, trying to find a reason for my suffering. I still had a semester left in my studies at Bethel, so instead of sending me on my way, the church offered to allow me to work on the maintenance staff. And not knowing what else to do, I took it. In a week's time, I went from pastoral leadership to scrubbing toilets; all the while studying theology and the Bible – a difficult task to say the least during a time of personal and spiritual anguish.

Over the course of that year, I tried to save my marriage while also trying to wrap my mind around a broken life. It didn't make sense to me that something like this could happen to someone devoting his life to ministry. Isn't God supposed to relieve pastors of this kind of heartache? My pain and confusion quickly turned into anger. Many nights, driving in the car, I would cry out to God, begging, even demanding, that He make things right again. But my circumstances never changed.

I had been away from church for several months as a subtle protest to God for what He allowed to happen in my life. Prior to taking the pastoral position, I was a part of another church community. And one day, while working, I felt a prompting on my heart to go to church. In my mind I kept hearing the words, *I miss you, Mike, I want to see you;* and a vision of my old church kept surfacing. I reluctantly went, still hurt and confused.

When I walked into the doors, I felt uncomfortable. I questioned whether I had made a mistake in coming. I sat by myself and tried to avoid contact with those around me. But as the music played, my heart jumped in my chest. You see, years ago I had claimed a particular worship song to be "mine and God's song." Every time I heard it, every time I sang the words, I felt God's presence. Believe it or not, that night, the worship band started playing that very song. I sang the words, and tears streamed down my face. I heard the voice in my mind speak again: *I know none of this makes any sense, but I still love you*. In that moment, I experienced an incredible sense of love. There's simply no way of explaining how peculiar it is to feel so much pain yet at the same time feel so much love, but that was how I felt.

That night was a turning point for me. Despite my entire world falling apart, I knew that God was enough for me. He was enough to keep breathing, to wake up each morning in order to see another day. In fact, He was the very air in my lungs. And seeing the smiling face of my little girl was just another reminder that perhaps God has a plan for me to positively impact the life of my daughter for as long as possible.

Years later, my broken road in life led to an old friend, and I was blessed to fall in love again. Life can be a mess sometimes, but God has the power to work within each of our messy lives and bring about something absolutely beautiful. And He did exactly that when I met my wife, Kristin.

I had wrestled with God and life. And even though I would never want to relive what I went through, I am nevertheless thankful for that period of wrestling as it became transformational for my faith. That is, my faith, my relationship with God, is the strongest it has ever been on account of the wrestling I went through. And it's interesting too, because it reminds me of what God proclaims to Jacob in the Bible. He says, "Your name will no longer be Jacob, but Israel, because you have struggled with God and with humans and have overcome" (Genesis 32:28). How incredible! Our wrestling with God and life can deliver an overall identity change, an identity which offers closeness and deeper intimacy with God!

Now, this doesn't mean that we should seek out suffering in order to grow in intimacy with God. This means that suffering, to some degree, will inevitably occur simply by living. It's part of life in a fallen world. So when suffering occurs, take hold of God and lean on Him. And as you wrestle, know that the potential for deeper intimacy with God awaits.

## *Romans 8:28*

There's a scripture verse many Christians are familiar with. It reads: "And we know that in all things God works for the good of those who love him, who have been called according to his purpose" (Romans 8:28). While some have tried to make this verse say something that it doesn't, I think God's work and ability to bring about good out of evil is important. In fact, it is part of the very heart of the faith of a wrestler. God is with us in our suffering. He is doing what only He can do; and that is to turn times of suffering into destinations of hope. He is drawing us out of our circumstances and pulling us closer to Him.

Romans 8:28 is not a promise that bad things won't happen to God's people, or that God somehow desires for us to be in our places of suffering in order to bring about His divine plan. Romans 8:28 is a promise that He is Immanuel, "God with us." And it's a promise that He has the power to bring about good from our times of suffering. It's a promise that He is always working on our behalf.

THEY'RE JUST NOT
INTERESTED

# CHAPTER 8

# THE PASSION OF THE CHRIST

One of the most impactful films in recent times is arguably *The Passion of the Christ*. From a personal standpoint, and setting aside criticisms that some in the Christian community might have for this film, I believe its portrayal of the pain and suffering that Jesus endured on His journey to the cross to be very heart-wrenching and effective. With that said, for years I had been curious about the word "passion" in its description of Jesus' journey toward death on the cross. I suppose I recognized the emotional aspect of what he endured, but it wasn't until sometime recently that I recognized that this word in reference to Jesus' mission to the cross carries significant meaning for us.

Sometime ago I was watching an interview with a highly regarded college wrestling coach. The coach was answering the interviewer's question regarding what approach he takes in order to keep his wrestlers focused and passionate about the sport despite the grind of the season. And after the coach explained what he does, the interviewer turned to the word and meaning of "passion," which he pointed out refers to, in the ancient Greek language, *suffering* and *enduring*. The coach is an outspoken Christian, and so he went on to explain this word in reference to Jesus (i.e., the passion of the Christ). That is, the passion of Jesus was defined by what He was passionate *about* as well as what He was *willing to suffer and endure* in order to accomplish the goal of His passion. In other words, Jesus was (and is) *passionate* for us – "For God so love the world that He gave His one and only Son" (John 3:16). And His passion was evidenced by what He was willing to suffer and endure in order to accomplish the purpose for His passion. In wrapping up the interview, the coach explained that this understanding of passion is crucial to the sport of wrestling. Most wrestlers enter college with a communicated passion for the sport. But when it comes down to it, passion for something is defined by what he or she is willing to suffer and endure for it. "My job," said the coach, "is to help these wrestlers remember why they love the sport, why they are passionate about it."

Isn't this reflective of the Christian faith? In other words, isn't it more about passion as modeled by Christ than it is about acquiring rational certainties or strict adherence to religious doctrine? Isn't it about our growing in relationship with Jesus to the point that we are willing to endure whatever hardships of life come upon us and not lose our faith in Him? Isn't it about continuing to trust and chase after Him? It seems to me that Christ's *passion* for us in His mission to the cross should be a reflection of our *passion* for Him. Jesus Himself states, "Whoever wants to be my disciple must deny themselves and take up their cross and follow me" (Matthew 16:24; Luke 9:23; Mark 8:34).

## *The Passion of the Wrestler*

Sticking with the sport of wrestling, in that I believe it offers a great picture relative to this topic, I'm reminded of a recent experience I had watching the Minnesota State wrestling tournament. My wife doesn't much care for the sport. And while I would of course love it if she did, I can understand that it's not appealing at the moment. It's a different kind of sport – grueling and somewhat painful to watch, especially if you're familiar with the wrestlers battling it out on the mat. So I went to the Xcel Center to watch the finals of the Minnesota State Wrestling tournament alone while my wife stayed home with the kids. It was there that I saw something very intriguing. I had seen it every year at the tournament but hadn't given it much thought in the past. That is, the tears which come from wrestlers after both victory and defeat. I was sitting in the stands, and two rows in front of me, I saw a young wrestler embrace his father after losing in the finals just minutes earlier. He buried his face in his father's shoulder and wept while his father held him tight and comforted him as best he could. In that same moment, I looked down at the arena floor and saw a wrestler, after just winning a state championship, bury his face in his hands and begin weeping as well. Two wrestlers with a face full of tears. For one of them, the tears were delivered on account of heartache. For the other, the tears were an expression of sincere happiness upon accomplishing his goal.

We've already noted the meaning of passion; that it involves not just a powerful emotional thrust toward something but also suffering and endurance. In other words, to be *passionate* about something is not merely reflective of how much a person loves or values it but how much he or she is willing to sacrifice and suffer for it. True passion is evident in one's continued commitment despite adversity.

When it comes to the sport of wrestling, it's easy to love and enjoy it when he or she is winning. All the hard work is paying off positively in their favor. But commitment to it simply on account of winning wouldn't necessarily be reflective of *passion*. Passion is evident in wrestlers when they maintain a commitment to the sport even when positive results are not apparent, even when confronted with disappointment. When things aren't going as planned, when faced with defeat, is wrestling worth it?

Nevertheless, it's the *tears* of wrestlers which seem to be the clearest indication of passion. The wrestler who loses may deliver tears of sadness because his or her sacrifice and suffering resulted in losing what he or she passionately trained for. The wrestler who wins may deliver tears of joy because his or her sacrifice and suffering resulted in achieving what he or she passionately trained for.

## *To Live*

Another important element of passion relates to the fact that it enables us to act on our desires. Passion requires action. If we are truly passionate about something, we cannot stand idle. Another way to put this is that the Christian faith is meant to impact the way in which we live. Pastor and theologian, Greg Boyd, writes, "...while the certainty-seeking model of faith is *psychological* in nature, the biblical concept is *covenantal*. That is, while the former is focused on a person's *mental state*, the latter is focused on how a person demonstrates a commitment by how they *live*"[17] (emphasis original).

This is true for any relationship. Relationships require us to take action in order to maintain and grow them. What's more is that relationships impact our

---

[17] Gregory A. Boyd, *Benefit of the Doubt: Breaking the Idol of Certainty*

decision-making. It's not just a matter of thinking; it's matter of doing. The Christian faith is not just a matter of changing a person's mind; it's a matter of changing the way in which they live. And the question is: Is Jesus worth this change in living? Is our faith in Him worth it despite the obvious struggles of life? Are we living with passion for Jesus? Is He worth our suffering and endurance?

# THEY'RE JUST NOT INTERESTED

# CHAPTER 9

# LAMENT

Walter Brueggemann in *The Psalms and the Life of Faith* delves into the issue of lament relative to Jewish, theological reflection. In simplistic terms, lament refers to an expression of grief or sorrow. But according to Brueggemann, lament "manifests Israel at its best, giving authentic expression to *the real experiences of life*"[18] (emphasis original). Within this is a recognition that the actual experiences of life matter, that a relationship with God is not simply a spiritual one but one that is holistic. It brings to the surface the reality of covenant relationship; that within a covenant relationship is the necessity of dialogue – the voice of God and the voice of His people. It demands that both voices are being heard, and requires response and faithfulness from both parties.

---

[18] Walter Brueggemann, *The Psalms and the Life of Faith* (Minneapolis, MN: Fortress Press, 1995).

For the Jew, the holistic nature of covenant relationship with God is understood. It was never thought that God's salvation pertained strictly to spiritual terms. God's interaction with humanity involved all of life – spiritual, political, economic, and so forth. And because of this, petition for His faithfulness to the covenant with His people involved far more than *spiritual* change and renewal. In the Jewish understanding of covenant, and one that is reflective of biblical faith, God can be questioned on grounds of social hardship, on issues pertaining to the physical world. In fact, to even voice lament regarding circumstances of physical and social suffering towards Him is a healthy sustaining of the divine relationship. It is effective practice of covenant relationship. While the previous two chapters brought to the fore the legitimacy of recognizing the fallenness of this world, our wrestling with it, and God by our side through it all, the concept of lament offers the aspect of dialogue, of actual *communication* with God in the midst of it.

Brueggemann discusses the loss that takes place when lament is absent, when we lose this dialogue and lose sight of the truth of the holistic nature of our relationship with God. One loss that results is the loss of *genuine covenant interaction*. The absence of lament "makes a religion of coercive obedience the only possibility."[19] This, however, is contrary to biblical faith. Biblical faith

---

[19] Walter Brueggemann, *The Psalms and the Life of Faith*

involves conversation and communion. And within this conversation and communion transpires genuine obedience, which is not a contrived need to please, but a genuine, yielding commitment.

Another loss caused by the absence of lament is the *stifling of the question of theodicy* – the capacity to raise questions of justice in terms of social goods, social access, and social power. In other words, theodicy involves trying to understand the heart of God within a world filled with evil. And without lament, without the ability to voice our struggle and our wrestling with the fallenness of this world, it's suggested that this world and our struggles simply don't matter. What's worse, the absence of lament suggests that our relationship with God is indifferent to the real matters of life. Brueggemann writes something very similar, and does so much more eloquently:

> Where the lament is absent, the normal mode of the theodicy question is forfeited. When the lament form is censured, justice questions cannot be asked and eventually become invisible and legitimate…Where the cry is not voiced heaven is not moved and history is not initiated. The end is hopelessness. Where the cry is seriously voiced, heaven may answer and earth may have a new chance. The new resolve in heaven and the

new possibility on earth depend on the initiation of protest.[20]

All in all, lament implies that communication, that genuine dialogue between God and His people is a legitimate aspect of our relationship with God; especially given the fact that the relationship/faith of the biblical type is covenantal. A covenant made between two parties requires communication from both.

Christianity, as biblical faith, as one which recognizes a reality moved and shaped by our relationship with God, must take seriously the above reflections. To suggest that our faith is completely separate from the real matters of life is to suggest that God is separate from the joys and hardships of human affairs, that God is indifferent to the human experience. But as we have uncovered with Jesus, and for example, the temptation story, we know that God is far from indifferent from the human experience. In fact, He took the human experience upon Himself. Also, the "Lord's prayer," the very supplication Jesus teaches us in the scriptures is an acknowledgement of God's concern for the human experience:

Our Father in heaven,

Hallowed by your name,

---

[20] Walter Brueggemann, *The Psalms and the Life of Faith*

*Your kingdom come,*

*Your will be done,*

*On earth as it is in heaven...*(Matthew 6:9-10, emphasis mine).

## *Personal versus Privatized Faith*

A leading notion within American Christianity is the belief that a relationship with God through Jesus Christ is reflective of one that is primarily personal. And *it is* primarily personal in terms of an individual's response and embrace of this relationship. As mentioned before, the gospel is a personal response to a personal calling. However, *personal* faith does not entail *private* faith. It must never be the case that God is privatized. *God is personal but never private.* If God is not personal, there is little meaning to faith. It merely becomes a philosophy or a set of religious teaching. Without a personal God, there is no personal dimension to belief; there is no relational God, no redemption, salvation, grace, or forgiveness, no power that can really change our lives beyond mere self-improvement. Denying the public God is a denial of biblical faith.

God is concerned and involved in human affairs. His influence in our lives is not merely spiritual, nor merely physical. His influence pervades the entirety of our being. Does this mean God is concerned with making His people materially wealthy, or that He is in the job of making sure America continues to stand atop the world economy? Of course not! But it does mean that He cares about the joys and hardships we experience in this life. It means that He cares about our place in life and what we are dealing with when we embrace Him in relationship. It means that He lends an open ear to our venting and frustrations about why life is the way it is at times, and that He personally takes on our pain and suffering. It means that God is with us in our wrestling with life's difficulties and He is encouraging us to maintain faith in His promise that He is working on our behalf and that He will one day redeem us and all of creation. One day evil and injustice will be no more. God's salvation through Jesus Christ is real, it's all-encompassing. It will one day overcome all that we lament about. His love and salvation will wipe away every tear we have shed in this life.

You see, God cares about your role as a father, mother, husband, wife, brother, sister, friend, athlete, student, employee, manager, or even your role as a politician. He cares about whatever role you engage in this life, how you interact with others, and every single struggle you face. He cares about what you go through in order to be all that you can be in each of these important roles in life, and more: the conflict, the embarrassments, the mistakes, the financial hardships, the sicknesses, the triumphs, and the times of great joy. God cares about every facet of your life, and He is with you through all of it: molding and shaping your heart into one that reflects the heart of Christ. Your faith in Jesus Christ should have a direct impact on how you approach life. Faith in Christ is personal, yes; but it's not something to keep private. It was never intended to be.

## *"Keep Your Faith in the Home and in the Church"*

When I wrote and published the book *Faith and Wrestling: How the Role of a Wrestler Mirrors the Christian Life* it was well received by many readers. However, there were a few people who were outspoken in their disdain for it. For them, Christianity in particular and religious faith in general, should be kept private. The book was different from this current one, in that it was much more geared toward the sport of wrestling and how the aspects of the sport that make it so unique and powerful are aspects shared with the Christian faith. In other words, we can utilize the imagery of the wrestling competitor and his- or her experience in the sport as a model for our life as followers of Jesus. However, by merely associating Christianity with the sport of wrestling, there were a few critics who wanted to expose the book as religious garbage. I received an e-mail from one of these critics (who, by the way, had not read the book), and in this e-mail he accused me of spreading religious propaganda about how a Christian wrestler is supposedly a better or more accomplished competitor on account of being a Christian. I of course explained to him that his accusation was inaccurate and that the book is merely correlating unique elements of the sport that are shared with a personal faith in Christ. His response: "Keep your faith in the home and in the church."

This issue of 'personal but not privatized' faith is a difficult one for nonbelievers to understand. But they need to recognize that religious faith, especially Christianity, is not something privatized. It's not simply a category of interest or something that can be tucked away and obtained when or if needed. The Christian faith, by nature of its relational component, impacts the way in which people approach life. They live differently on account of it. Does that mean they are better people or necessarily more moral? Not really. Every person who takes a step of faith in Jesus Christ takes that step from a unique place or position in life. And God isn't in the work of magic transformations, either. A life successfully and consistently reflecting God's goodness is a lifelong process.

The truth is that we are all naturally selfish. A life reflective of God's goodness is selfless; it's self-sacrificial. We are selfish and often utilize our leaning toward selfishness in order to protect ourselves in times of difficulty or conflict. But when the love of Christ has confronted a human life, it begins to transform that life – slowly but surely ridding it of selfishness and restoring it with selflessness. For some, the process of this exchange, of this transformation, is a lot easier, in that some people are naturally less selfish than others. Every human being is unique, and their relationship with Christ is unique. Every human being embraces Christ from a place in life filled with their own set of issues.

Those who are open to spirituality but who reject the Christian faith also need to recognize this element of personal faith that is not privatized. True faith is not something to compartmentalize or only dabble with. This means that one's Christian faith is going to impact both the smallest and biggest decisions. It's not just some semi-spiritual aid to help parents raise moral children, or some self-help guide to being a "better" person. The Christian faith is something which impacts life itself.

It's absolutely true that Christians have performed injustice in the name of God. This is an unfortunate reality that stands alongside all the good that Christians have done in the world. Also, in America, both liberal and conservative Christians have served as loud and obnoxious voices in the political realm. Both are guilty of expressing their religious convictions inappropriately as it pertains to political opinion and legislation. But be that as it may, the mistakes and failures of Christian people are not indicators of anything except imperfect human beings who still have the obvious capability to make mistakes and fail despite the truth of their faith. The truth of Christianity is not founded on the deeds or misdeeds of Christian people; it's founded on the life, death and resurrection of Jesus Christ.

    Those who are open to spirituality but who lack any interest in the Christian faith will probably never find their interest increasing on account of Christian people. If they reject the faith on account of their dislike for Christian people, then their thoughts or feelings about the faith may likely never change. But, again, that's not the issue. Embracing the Christian faith is not a response to Christian people. Embracing the Christian faith is a response to Jesus Christ.

THEY'RE JUST NOT
INTERESTED

# CHAPTER 10

# THE BEAUTY OF SIMPLICITY

If I were to try and summarize everything I have written throughout this book in a short and concise statement, I suppose I would suggest that *God brings simplicity to a world of people stuck in a merry go round of complexity.* But even though the statement seems to be accurate, it demands explanation, which is of course why I couldn't just publish the above sentence and ask for your money.

It's true, even though our hearts yearn for simplicity, simplicity nevertheless makes us uncomfortable. As a result, we turn relatively simple matters into complex ones. Just consider this from a religious standpoint. What once began as a simple yet profound gospel message has turned into a complex, religious system. Even in Jesus' arrival onto the scene, there was already the established system of Judaism. He came and immersed Himself into an ancient, religious culture with long held theology and systems of belief. But rather than embrace the complexity of Jewish religion and culture, He completely disrupted it. He, for example, took all 613 Jewish laws and boiled them down to 2: Love God and love others. And when He brought salvation, He didn't offer a system of law or doctrine; He offered Himself...He offered relationship.

Now, the development of Christian theology and doctrine after the ascension of Christ was somewhat necessary, for sure. That is, in order to survive on this side of heaven, it was important for Christianity not to disappear into obscurity. In fact, ironically, Christianity began to incorporate complexity as a result of the faith being stripped of its simplicity early on by humans doing what they do best: complicate things. For instance, pseudo-Christian movements distorted the faith with their own set of incoherent complexities; and opponents of the faith were delivering complex philosophical challenges. But the church, over the centuries, became so infatuated with theology and doctrine-making that what we're now left with is a very complex system of religion. And so today, Christians and non-Christians alike need to sift through all the philosophical and theological noise in order to find the heart of the gospel, in order to find Jesus. But of course the beauty of simplicity is that Jesus is there, so it's worth the labor.

I'm not here to suggest that theology and doctrine are a waste of time. I think I have been pretty consistent in stating that I believe they are important. In fact, theology can be a form of worship when delivered with humility and care. But the moment we start applying salvific qualities to "right theology" or "right doctrine" is the moment we have made an idol in place of Christ.

## *When Theology is Useless*

I walked into my "senior seminar" class with a sense of confidence and relief. I had taken a considerably long route to my college degree, but I was finally entering the final stage. Also, I would be lying if I said I didn't think I had climbed the ladder of theological prestige throughout my academic journey, and the top of the ladder appeared to be within view. I had worked hard, stretched my mind to its capacity, and now it was time to flex my theological muscle.

Dr. Ezigbo (who preferred to be called Victor) offered a statement at the beginning of the course that has stuck with me ever since. "Okay, class, first of all, congratulations for making it this far. You've worked really hard throughout your studies here, and now you're going to put all of your knowledge to use in a project, a thesis paper, that will reflect something unique to your journey." Victor positioned himself in front of the class and looked at us intently. "But as you work throughout the semester, it's very important that you keep this in mind. The only theology worth doing is theology which connects to an issue that people in your community actually care about. This could be an issue in the world community, in our particular society or culture, or in individual church communities, but it must be something pertaining to theology that people are actually concerned or asking about. It must be relevant. If they are not interested in the subject you're thinking of writing and theologizing about, then don't do it. It's useless."

I sat back in my chair. I thought about all the stuff I had been enamored with, the stuff of theology that most people don't really care about anymore: Luther's 'theology of the cross,' Karl Barth and the neo-orthodox movement of 'dialectical theology' in the mid-twentieth century, whether or not the liberal protestant, Friedrich Schleiermacher, was really that bad after all, or how to discern between orthodox and heretical views of Trinitarian theology. All of it was essentially useless despite engaging in these complex matters for reasons of personal interest and speculation.

It was then that I realized theology is more purposeful than merely a subject of fascination or a resource for intellectual value. Theology is meant to draw people to the love and worship of God. In other words, theology should be a resource with which to help people understand better – however much as possible – the heart of God. And it should also serve as a reminder of the sheer 'otherness' of God: His glory and goodness. What's more is that there are issues unique to specific places in time. While there are certainly questions that have followed humanity, there are nevertheless a great many questions that are new and that are a response to circumstances of a unique place in time. In other words, as we move forward, society, culture, and technology change. New problems arise. And theology allows us the opportunity to contemplate God and life in the midst of it all.

     I learned something else by the end of the class that semester and the completion of my thesis paper. That is, all the theologizing we perform should deliver us back to the cornerstone of Christian thought: Jesus Christ. Yes, it's simplistic, perhaps even annoyingly so for those who desire a more complex pursuit. But without Jesus, there is no Christian theology.

## *It Can't Be that Simple*

     For whatever reason, we can't seem to find comfort in the simplicity of the gospel. Whether standing within the church or looking in from the outside, we struggle to fathom that the meaning of life and our entrance into eternity is embodied in the person of Jesus Christ. So we turn the gospel message of salvation into a system of religion. Maybe our tendency toward complexity is a product of our desire to be in control of our destiny. Simply leaving our salvation in the hands of Christ has us thinking that this is only half the truth, that there must be more to it. Resting in the grace of God is a lot more difficult than it sounds, because it means letting go of our natural reflex toward control which inevitably breeds complexity which only leads to more confusion.

The vast number of Christian denominations is largely a result of Christians unable to find rest in the simplicity of the gospel. They challenged one another in terms of what they perceived to be proper doctrine and eventually separated from one another. Thankfully, God is bigger than our tendency toward complexity, and He has been able to draw people to Himself from every corner of the earth despite it.

The faith of a wrestler is a faith which seeks to find rest in the beautiful simplicity of God's grace; a grace revealed in the gospel of Jesus Christ.

## THEY'RE JUST NOT INTERESTED

# CHAPTER 11

# THIS LIFE MATTERS

Throughout the course of this book I have tried to describe not only the benefit of the faith of a wrestler, but how the faith of a wrestler is the biblically grounded faith we should be approaching others with. Whether I have been successful in this is up to the reader to decide. But while the previous chapters have focused more on us as Christians in terms of rediscovering our faith, this particular chapter I would like to focus more on what we are communicating to nonbelievers, particularly those who are open to spirituality but who lack any interest in the Christian faith.

## *"What Does This Have to Do with my Life Now?"*

For quite some time, American, evangelical Christianity has promulgated a belief of "going to heaven when we die." In other words, when engaging others with the gospel, we have typically run with the approach of trying to help people consider the following question: "Where do you think you'll end up when you die – heaven or hell?"

While the question is important to consider, in that we should be concerned about life in eternity, what we end up doing is suggesting that this present life doesn't matter, that all that really matters is whether or not we have obtained our golden ticket to heaven.

I remember talking with a young man about the gospel, and after patiently listening to my longwinded explanation about Jesus and salvation, he kindly asked me, "Okay, that's all very interesting, but what does this have to do with my life now?"

His question was a great one! It made me realize that we have focused so heavily on this notion of making sure we obtain our ticket to heaven, that we have forgotten an equally important issue: what does Christianity mean for our lives now? Our standard response has been to live a moral or Godly life. But what does this mean? In other words, how does this impact our lives as husbands, wives, fathers, mothers, brothers, sisters, employees, and so on. Because if living a moral life is merely reflective of abstaining from sin, then we're actually a bit stuck when it comes to living this life, and living it well. In other words, abstaining from sin is a passive approach. What about the active component?

## *It's time for a History Lesson*

Despite the popular use of questions pertaining to "going to heaven when we die," I want to suggest that this is probably not the best approach, and it's not really even Christian. In order to understand what I'm getting at, it's important to turn back in history to the early church.

One of the first opponents to Christianity early on was that of Gnosticism. Gnosticism was a pseudo-Christian movement which attempted to completely spiritualize Christian belief. It involved a wide range of thoughts; but as a general rule, its emphasis on spirituality was a prime component. For instance, gnostic belief viewed *matter (nature)* as *evil* and *spirit* as *good*. Therefore, the resurrection of Jesus was believed (within this group) not to be a *physical* resurrection but a purely *spiritual* one. In fact, salvation in this mode of belief was an *escape* from the physical body and the present world. That is, heaven and earth were believed to comprise two separate realms, completely detached from one another. So what Jesus was believed to offer in His coming was a way in which to escape the world. *This* is where the notion of "going to heaven when we die" finds its beginnings. It's not Christianity; it's philosophical dualism. It's not Christianity; it's Gnosticism. And it is a notion that found added encouragement in Enlightenment thought.

Far from the idea that the goal of the Christian faith is *escaping* this world and entering into heaven, the actual goal is *redemption*. Jesus is not in the work of helping us escape God's creation. He is in the work of redeeming us in the course of His grand redemption of *all* of creation. Remember, when God created, He deemed it good (Genesis 1). And when sin perverted His good creation, God's response was not, "I must implement a means for escape." When sin perverted His good creation, God's response was, "I will redeem my creation and make it good again, starting with humanity."

So what does all this matter in the grand scheme of things? Well, to be honest, this dualistic thinking (escaping earth and going to heaven) impacts the way in which we approach the world. Even worse, *it affects the way in which we communicate our Christian faith.* Not only is escapism a distortion of the gospel, but belief steeped in escapism is not really something people in our American culture are interested in. Our American culture is deeply existential. That is, people care about the here and now. They are interested in things that will have an impact on their lives *now*. As difficult as life can be at times, most people in our culture aren't exactly looking for an escape. They're looking for fulfillment. They're looking to be redeemed. Just think about how our society deals with evil (or injustice). When confronted with injustice, we band together. We create a social movement for change. The idea is hardly ever to escape. The idea is to rid what is bad in the course of redeeming what is good. The process is founded on genuine belief in hope – hope that, with perseverance, things will get better.

In 2012, New Testament scholar, N.T. Wright, came out with a book titled, *How God Became King*. In this book, Wright suggests that we have essentially failed to recognize the gospel *within* the gospel. In other words, the message within the gospel narratives is not about going to heaven when we die. The gospel is about God reclaiming His creation (His kingdom, if you will), and through the person of Jesus, redeeming the world unto Himself. This means, for example, that the gospel is not about obtaining moral correction in order to be made right for heaven. While moral living is a byproduct of following Jesus, creating moral people suited for heaven is not the goal of the Christian faith. The goal is to be a part of God's grand story of redemption, to be a part of His kingdom, to be a part of His eternal family.

So instead of communicating to nonbelievers that to be a Christian is to be moral and to go through a process of being suited for an escape to heaven, we should be communicating a message of hope, of family, of being redeemed in the here and now, of wrestling with all of life's issues, of making the world a better place. The Bible talks about being transformed in the now – in *this* life – and that leaving this life is simply a transition into eternity. After all, that's why Jesus teaches us to pray God's "kingdom come, [His] will be done, on earth as it is in heaven" (Matthew 6:10). The goal is not to escape earth but instead to *bring heaven to earth.*

    This certainly doesn't leave out the spiritual component to the Christian faith. To embrace God through Jesus is truly a remarkable spiritual experience. But the objective of Christianity is not to help people make their escape for heaven. Is there a heaven upon our exit from earth? The Bible suggests that there is. But according to the Bible, God will *renew* heaven and earth, and with what is left, create something new (2 Peter 3:13; Revelation 21:1). And this renewed place is our true destination.

    You see, one of the primary reasons why the spiritually open are not interested in the Christian faith is because they actually care about this life and their role it. They feel as if most Christians are too 'heavenly minded to do any earthly good.' They feel as if Christians are so caught up in their future spiritual state of being that they've lost any sort of genuine care for this present life. But obviously, if they got to know even the most charismatic of Christians, they would find that such an accusation is completely false. Most Christians do care about this life, and they want to make the most of it. The problem, of course, is that this is not what is communicated.

The truth is: the spiritually open *need* Jesus, not because they need to punch their ticket to heaven, not because they need to be infused with moral correction, but because Jesus brings true life. He brings true life in this present world. He brings hope, meaning and purpose to this world. Salvation is not merely something that occurs when we take our last breath; salvation is something that occurs the moment a person accepts the invitation of Jesus and allows Him into their life. Salvation is here. Salvation is now.

## *Consider the Cost*

While we as a Christian community want to present the gospel better to those who are spiritually open or seeking, we also want to be honest. So if the faith of a wrestler truly is an accurate reflection of Christianity, then let's be honest: It's tough; it's a battle! If a comfortable religious faith is what they're looking for, then Christianity is not for them.

In Luke 14:28-30, Jesus says, "Suppose one of you wants to build a tower. Won't you first sit down and estimate the cost to see if you have enough money to complete it? For if you lay the foundation and are not able to finish it, everyone who sees it will ridicule you, saying, 'This person began to build and wasn't able to finish.'" Jesus is using an example pertaining to financial cost in order to communicate that potential followers of Him should take seriously the decision and commitment they are making. To follow Jesus is not a lackadaisical choice. They need to consider the cost and really know what they're committing to. And remember, prior to this Jesus already described the cost in following Him: "Whoever wants to be my disciple must deny themselves and take up their cross daily and follow me" (Luke 9:23). This is not a faith of comfort. The Christian faith, though it offers true and eternal life, is also one of sacrifice.

Again, the Christian faith is not about God making moral people suited for heaven. But it is about God working in and through each person who has committed their life to Him; and this commitment bears significant, life-altering consequences. The goal is to transform each Christian's life so that it reflects the goodness of His Son, Jesus. This is a lifelong process, not a work of magic. Each Christian has a part to play in submitting to God's work in their lives. Sometimes there are terrible bumps in the road. Sometimes they experience setbacks. Sometimes their old self tries to rear its ugly, selfish head. But God honors a committed heart. He simply continues to work out every selfish piece of their heart and replaces each piece with humility and with His goodness and love.

The bottom line is that the Christian faith is not a faith for those seeking an easy and comfortable option for their spirituality. For most, it's tough. It's more like a constant wrestling match than anything else. But the foundation of the faith is built on Jesus Christ. It's personal in nature; and the truth embodied in the person of Jesus is too powerful to ignore once you've been confronted by it. Christ fulfills our deepest spiritual longings. Yet despite a life of fulfillment in Christ, we are not given the full picture of His redeeming plans. We are often left confused about why this or that happens, or left wondering where God is when life hits us with pain and suffering.

Even though we can't see the full picture, we are nevertheless given the spirit of Christ ("God with us"), and we are given glimpses of the magnificent world to come. We're given hope. We're offered a vision of the beauty that lies ahead. God helps us to see that we are a part of this grand story of His. For now, we're in this fallen world filled with its mixture of good and evil; and we're commanded to live this life to the fullest, set our sights on Him, and seek, at every moment, to bring heaven to the earth.

This life matters. As God is doing a good work in us, we are commanded to do a good work in the world; and in the process, make disciples of others. In other words, we are commanded by God to submit to the work He is doing in our lives, to do good in the world while He is active in our lives, and invite others into the family. Life eternal starts now.

## Nonreligious Acts for Heavenly Good

I think going to church, reading the Bible, partaking in acts of service for the poor and so on, are all important and wonderful things; but truth be told, I think seemingly nonreligious acts can produce far more heavenly good. Let me explain.

I shared a piece of my personal story regarding the downfall of my first marriage earlier in this book. Although I now have a wonderfully fulfilling life in my marriage with Kristin, the experience over the course of my divorce was nothing short of horrific and I would never wish it upon anybody. So when an acquaintance of mine revealed that he was struggling with his wife and that she was threatening with divorce, I believed that I had an obligation to be there for him and encourage him in any way I could. This didn't involve grabbing my Bible and delivering a sermon to him about marriage and God's desire for marital unity and faithfulness to the vows that were made. Instead, it involved responding to God's prompting on my heart to be present for this man, listen to him, and provide any encouragement I could in his struggle and his attempt to save his marriage. So that's exactly what I did. Though our conversations were not theological, God was present in our meetings. The fact that I responded to God's prompting on my heart, and was there for this man in his time of need, was more important and showed more of God's love than anything

"Christianly" I could have said to him. These meetings and conversations were very emotional at times, and it often seemed like our getting together was a lost cause. But I stuck with it, and so did he.

While this man's relationship with his wife isn't by any means free of troubles, their marriage is nevertheless still alive and they are both happy and working hard at remaining faithful to the vows that they made to each other. Moreover, I know that their two children will reap the benefit of an example of a marriage that stuck with it despite the most difficult of times.

You see, I wasn't practicing some religious ritual or even engaging in theological discourse about God's design for our lives when I met with this man. And yet, my nonreligious act (I believe) did far more heavenly good than any sort of religious initiative could have.

My best friend, Josh, did the same thing for me. When I was going through the separation from my ex-wife and the subsequent divorce, Josh was there for me. He saw me at my worst. He's a pastor; but even as a pastor, he knew that the best approach was not one which immediately inserted theology or the Bible, even when it may have seemed to him that I was potentially having a crisis of faith. Instead, Josh was present. He was loving and kind. And the love he expressed to me showed more of God than anything else he could have said to me. I often told Josh during that time that he was Christ to me, in that he allowed the love of Christ to shine through him in his love and care. I am eternally grateful for the love of Christ that shined brightly through Josh.

While both the aforementioned interactions involved one Christian to another, the truth is that the same approach should be taken in our interaction with nonbelievers. I heard a saying some time ago which states, "People don't care about what you know until they know that you care." Those who are open to spirituality don't care about what we (as Christians) know, or what we could share with them regarding God and the gospel of Jesus Christ, until they know that we care about them. It is far more important to engage in nonreligious encounters with others and show Christ's love through our actions than it is to confront them with religious philosophy or Christian theology.

While this method or approach might seem obvious, it's unfortunately highly ignored. Far too often Christians engage others by immediately speaking a foreign language of 'Christianity' and 'doctrine.' And what this does is only accentuate the existing caricatures and misconceptions of the Christian faith. Instead of engaging nonbelievers as human beings, we engage them with lofty arguments about God's existence, a god-man named Jesus, and a coming Day of Judgment in which God will be sending people to either heaven or hell. And while the people we are engaging might be open to spirituality, they're not willing to listen to us until they know that we actually care about them and that we actually care about the real circumstances of life.

## THEY'RE JUST NOT INTERESTED

# CONCLUSION

The message within this book has been on my heart for many years. However, it took a great deal of time, experience, and reflection in order to get to the core of what my heart had been discerning for so long. What ended up as a message for the church at large started out as merely a personal struggle. For me, it began in my early twenties, before starting my studies in theology at Bethel University, and wrestling with this whole idea of 'thinking correctly.'

I remember walking out of a Dairy Queen, and one of my friends mentioned something about a theological belief in Christianity called "calvinism." I hadn't heard of it, but his description of it as God exerting meticulous, divine control was interesting to me. It was suggested that free will (our *response* to God in particular) was imaginary, that God sovereignly elects certain people to be with Him in eternal heaven and sovereignly damns others to eternal hell.

Initially, I shrugged off the theological suggestion with an awkward laugh. But for the next several months, I went through a confusing and somewhat painful journey in order to discover the "truth" of the matter. I read the Bible with investigative fervor and read book after book written by both advocates and opponents of calvinism. Rather than finding psychological relief, I seemed to fall deeper and deeper into confusion. What's worse is that I was experiencing internal anguish as a result. One calvinist theologian I read even suggested that calvinism is simply a synonym for true Christian belief, and that belief in a God different than the calvinist type was worship of a false god. This was difficult for me, in that my heart yearned for God but my mind was stuck in a state of confusion. I began to entertain the idea that, if I failed to 'think correctly,' if I didn't have proper theology about God, I would be denied eternity in heaven with Him.

After several months stuck in limbo relative to the theological notion of calvinism, I decided that I needed to figure it out, once and for all, and make a decision. I went to church early one night, locked myself in one of the conference rooms, and read what is considered a highlight of scripture in calvinist theology: Romans 9. I had read this chapter in the Bible no short of a hundred times over the course of those months, and this was going to be my final attempt at resolving my mental dilemma on the matter. But after reading it yet again, my thinking, my theology, wasn't cured.

## THEY'RE JUST NOT INTERESTED

I walked into the sanctuary for the start of the service, and I did so with a heavy heart. I loved God so much, but my mind could not seem to find any relief. I feared for my eternal destiny.

As the music played during the worship portion of the service, and doing my best to sing praises to the God I love, I had had enough. With tears in my eyes, I whispered, "God, I don't care if you divinely chose me without any response of my own, or if I had a genuine choice in responding to your love and grace. All I care about is that I have a relationship with you. All I care about is that I love you."

As I released these words and surrendered them to God, I felt His powerful presence. My mind immediately felt relief. I no longer carried the mental burden that I had been carrying for several months. And from that day forward, I felt freedom to grow in my relationship with God like never before. I knew that my theology was important, but I also knew that my salvation, my relationship with God, was not dependent on it. Christ, and Christ alone, was my sole dependence.

Even prior to my confrontation with calvinism, I had long believed that proper thinking was necessary for anyone who embraced the Christian faith. It's what I was taught. But my personal experience of questioning my faith on account of a competing theology, allowed me to see a glimpse into the problems inherent in my faith at the time, as well as how I was communicating the Christian faith to others.

Again, I believe that theology and doctrine are important. But theology and doctrine are not the gospel. The gospel pertains to God's divine disruption of our world in the person of Jesus Christ and how this radically changes everything. The salvation of Jesus Christ is the cornerstone of life. And our response to Him holds everlasting consequences. What's more is that these consequences do not just pertain to some future heavenly destination. They involve life today. Salvation in Jesus Christ impacts all of life. Who we are and what we're doing today matters. And it's not strictly correlated to spiritual mumbo jumbo.

*This* is what we should be communicating to the spiritually open or seeking. The Christian faith is not about the bolstering of a religion or converting people to a religious walk of life. The Christian faith is about our response to Jesus Christ and the truth that He alone holds. It's about relationship with Him and the incredible and necessary transformation of our lives in order to reflect His goodness. It's about an opportunity to embrace the story that God is writing, one that is carrying creation to a magnificent end...an end that is, in reality, only the beginning.

The spiritually open or seeking are just not interested in Christianity. But perhaps it's because they haven't truly heard the 'good news' of Jesus. Perhaps it's because we needed to rediscover the Christian faith for ourselves first in order to effectively communicate God's magnificent message to the world.

The Christian faith isn't about who is the most theologically proficient or who can present the most doctrinally sound defense of their faith. The Christian faith looks like a wrestler. Faith is a relationship; and with a relationship comes struggle. God has empowered us to embrace this struggle and to serve as advocates of His redemption.

They're just not interested. But perhaps they will be.

## ABOUT THE AUTHOR

Michael Fessler is an author and speaker. He currently resides in Minnesota with his wife and two children. Prior to this book, Michael wrote and published *Faith and Wrestling: How the Role of a Wrestler Mirrors the Christian Life*. He has a B.A. in Biblical and Theological Studies from Bethel University, and an M.A. in Communications from Concordia University – Saint Paul.

Contact the author: Michael Fessler
mrfess@hotmail.com

Praise for *Faith and Wrestling: How the Role of a Wrestler Mirrors the Christian Life*

"The Bible tells us that believers are transformed by the renewing of their minds. Another way of putting this is …taking into captivity every thought to the obedience of Christ. This means learning how to think of all of life, including sport, from a biblical perspective. Michael Fessler's book is drenched in Christian worldview. Those who wrestle with its truths will be richer for it. I wish that I had been able to drink from its wisdom as a young man but am grateful to be able to do so as an old(er) one." – **Jack Spates**, MDiv, Baptist Bible College & Seminary, and former Head Wrestling Coach at the University of Oklahoma

"I can immediately relate to the things that Michael Fessler writes about in his book 'Faith and Wrestling'" Wrestling demands a high degree of commitment, perhaps more than any other sport. Therefore, the common temptation we face is to make wrestling our main source of significance. Michael helps us see the importance of allowing God to let us use wrestling as an act of worship of God, rather than making wrestling our God. He helps us see how the struggles we deal with in wrestling can help us in dealing with the spiritual battles that are a part of life. This book is an excellent resource for anyone working in the athletic world." – **John Peterson**, 1976 Olympic Champion

"My belief has always been that wrestling is a microcosm of life. Most of the things that we are going to experience in life are going to be experienced in a wrestling career. Michael does an excellent job in paralleling the relationship between faith and wrestling. His book expresses the importance of developing the total athlete—spiritually, physically, emotionally, and socially. I look forward to the day when people (including wrestlers) from 'every nation, tribe, people and language' will gather to worship our God. (Revelation 7:9, 11)." – **Gene Davis**, Director of Wrestling at Athletes in Action, and Bronze medalist in the 1976 Olympic Games

"Michael Fessler concisely captures the heart of a Christian wrestler pursuing God's glory. The book is captivating in combining biblical truths with real-life stories. You will be encouraged and inspired to think about the gospel as greater than athletic glory as Fessler explains the biblical basis for competing. Just as Fessler's approach to use wrestling as a tool for the gospel, we at Athletes in Action use the sport of wrestling to share the gospel around the world. I highly recommend this book to anyone who is passionate about their faith and the sport of wrestling." – **Rob Bronson**, International Wrestling Team Coordinator at Athletes in Action

"'Faith and Wrestling: How the Role of a Wrestler Mirrors the Christian Life'" provides a thoughtful, thought-provoking analysis of the interconnection between Christian faith and world's oldest and greatest sport that will speak to wrestlers, coaches, families and wrestling fans as they continue their own unique faith journeys." – **Intermatwrestle.com**

They're Just Not Interested: Rediscovering our Faith and Approaching Nonbelievers with the Faith of a Wrestler

By Michael Fessler

©2016

Made in the USA
San Bernardino, CA
13 December 2016